The Art of
INVESTIGATIVE
INTERVIEWING

The Art of
INVESTIGATIVE
INTERVIEWING

Third Edition

INGE SEBYAN BLACK, CPP, CFE, CPOI
CHARLES L. YESCHKE

AMSTERDAM • BOSTON • HEIDELBERG • LONDON
NEW YORK • OXFORD • PARIS • SAN DIEGO
SAN FRANCISCO • SINGAPORE • SYDNEY • TOKYO

Butterworth-Heinemann is an imprint of Elsevier

ELSEVIER

Acquiring Editor: Brian Romer
Development Editor: Keira Bunn
Project Manager: Priya Kumaraguruparan
Designer: Maria Inês Cruz

Butterworth-Heinemann is an imprint of Elsevier
225 Wyman Street, Waltham, MA 02451, USA
The Boulevard, Langford Lane, Kidlington, Oxford OX5 1GB UK

First edition 1997
Second edition 2003

Library of Congress Cataloging-in-Publication Data
Application submitted

British Library Cataloguing-in-Publication Data
A catalogue record for this book is available from the British Library

ISBN: 978-0-12-411577-4

For information on all Butterworth-Heinemann publications
visit our web site at store.elsevier.com

This book has been manufactured using Print On Demand technology. Each copy is
produced to order and is limited to black ink. The online version of this book will show color
figures where appropriate.

Working together
to grow libraries in
developing countries

www.elsevier.com • www.bookaid.org

I dedicate this book to my beloved 22-year-old daughter, Brittany Alexandra Larson, who was tragically and abruptly killed when she was thrown from her motorcycle and struck by another driver while in the process of being rescued by others, on June 6, 2012. This book is also dedicated to Brooke and Justin, my other two children, and my grandson, Ty.

Brittany is sadly missed by everyone who knew and loved her, especially me.

Brittany always believed in me and I will always remember how smart, passionate, and loving she was. Her free spirit and radiance will forever be my light.

MISSION STATEMENT

My goal is to help educate interviewers, even those who only occasionally participate in interviews. I encourage you to prepare for each interview as though it is the interview of your life, because maybe it will be. You might only have one chance to talk to your subject, so make it successful. I hope to help you learn to do that.

Inge Sebyan Black

CONTENTS

ACKNOWLEDGMENTS

I want to thank Larry Fennelly, who has been my friend and mentor for the past 30 years. Since 1982 we have served on the ASIS Crime Prevention and Loss Council together as well as President Reagan's Task Force on Rape and Violent Crime. Larry, president of Litigation Consultants Inc., is an expert witness and security consultant. Retired after 35 years as sergeant with the Harvard Police Department, Larry has written over 28 books on the subject of security and crime prevention. His guidance, knowledge, and expertise have been invaluable in my growth and expertise in the corporate security industry.

I also want to thank the following people:

Marianna Perry, training and development manager for Securitas Security Services, previously director of the National Crime Prevention Institute and the Kentucky State Police

John O'Rourke, CPP, security consultant, previously with the New Jersey State Police

Joe Ditsch, Attorney with Fowler Law Firm in Minneapolis, Minnesota, who provided insight on the ethics chapter

Raymond Andersson, who provided the Australasian Code of Conduct, endorsed in the spring of 2013, by the Australasian Council of Security Professionals

Louis A. Tyska, CPP, past president of ASIS and former investigator with Pinkerton Detective Agency, for writing the forward with Larry Fennelly

Pat Clawson, private investigator and former investigative reporter for CNN and NBC News. Pat has been a friend for years and I am grateful for his contribution of the Preface to this book.

I also want to thank my dearest friends, Holly Higgs, Pat Morris, and Greg Carlson, for their love and support over the past three decades.

Inge is the Minnesota Manager for Apollo International, based in Walpole, MA. Apollo, providing Uniformed Services, Security Consulting and Investigation Services.

Inge earned her BA in Criminal Justice, along with her Law Enforcement Degree, both from Metropolitan State University in St. Paul, Minnesota.

Inge's security career started in 1977, joining ASIS International in 1983. Inge earned both her CPP (Certified Protection Professional) and CPO (Certified Protection Officer) in 1994 and CPO. In 2008, Inge became a CPOI (Certified Protection Officer Instructor). Inge is a licensed Private Investigator in the State of Minnesota and has also held her license in Quebec and Ontario Canada. She earned her CFE (Certified Fraud Examiner) in 1995 and in 2000 earned designation as a Certified Emergency Manager by both FEMA and the State of Minnesota.

For the past 35 years, Inge has worked in both the corporate and private security field, conducting interviews and investigations involving fraud, external and internal theft, corporate espionage, embezzlement, and workplace issues, including workplace violence and harassment. Inge successfully obtained hundreds of confessions for prosecution, knowing the criticality of preparation and the value of documentation. Her interviewing skills are a critical component when contracted for security risk assessments. Inge has conducted security and threat risk assessments for both government properties and private corporations in both the United States and Canada. Besides investigations, she also conducts security audits, writes security/investigation policies and procedures, conducts Security Analysis, supervises investigation units and consults on physical security.

Inge is a certified security trainer in the state of Minnesota and has trained security personnel in the areas of investigations, contract security management, emergency planning, and physical security audits. She has been a security management instructor at St. Paul Technical College and Pine Technical College, both in Minnesota.

Inge started serving on ASIS International committees early on when, in 1983, she served on the Educational Committee as well as President Reagan's Rape and Violent Crime Committee. In 2008, until 2013, she served on the Physical Security Council. Currently Inge serves as Chair for the Crime Prevention and Loss Prevention Council, through ASIS International.

Inge has been one of the speakers at ASIS International conferences since 1983. While serving as a council member on the Physical Security Council for the past 5 years, Inge served as Chair for the sub-committee on Security Force Management in 2009 and 2010, organizing, leading and speaking at the ASIS's workshops on Security Force Management.

She has co-authored many publications on security such as; security personnel selection, personnel deployment, handling complaints and grievances, workplace violence and domestic violence.

It has been said that when an investigator finds herself in a position of working on an investigation, it's like working a math problem backward. There are several phases that comprise phases in an investigation. These phases are reports taken, photographs taken, forensics gathered, and all the data assigned to an investigative team. After a considerable amount of time spent gathering additional evidence, interviews, and statements collected, the legwork has been completed and hopefully the criminals or suspects have been identified as well as located. After being arrested and Mirandized, they are processed. They then are either released on bail or perhaps indicted by a grand jury, incarcerated, or given instructions to appear. As investigators with more than 30 years' experience, we have learned that it is our goal to obtain admissions or a confession in this process.

The title of this book is apt: *The Art of Investigation and Interviewing.* The subject is an art form composed of a combination of psychology and sociology, but most of all, street smarts. Cases rarely have eyewitnesses who come forward and state, "I saw the suspect commit the crime. I know who he is and where he lives."

At times you have been faced with a very complex investigation that has an enormous amount of diverse evidence to be reviewed. The 2013 Boston Marathon bombings is such an example. Numerous hours of professional video and amateur cell phone video and photos had to be combed through. Reporters conducted interviews with victims, witnesses, and authorities, all of this being broadcast and published. At the same time there was evidence to be gathered and catalogued, DNA gathered and safeguarded, and the chain of evidence logged and controlled. Of course, we also had to go thorugh the process of identifying all witnesses and information documented throughout the stages of the investigation with statements taken and reports made.

Inge Sebyan Black has done a terrific job with this third edition of Charles Yeschke's book. Students of investigations will learn much from this text. We believe that most of the crimes that have been solved were successful due to proper investigative and interviewing protocols. We highly recommend this book, which documents all the acceptable procedures detailed in Ms. Black's rewrite.

Lawrence J. Fennelly
Litigation Consultants Inc.

Louis A. Tyska, CPP
Past President of ASIS and former investigator,
Pinkerton Detective Agency

This wonderful book, *The Art of Investigative Interviewing*, is a classic and timeless reference work that belongs in every investigator's library. I am humbled and grateful to write the introduction for this new edition. Past editions have enriched my life and professional prowess. I am certain this new edition will do the same for you.

Over my 40-plus years of experience as a network TV investigative reporter, major-market radio talk show host, and private investigator, I have interviewed a remarkable cross-section of society: presidents, senators, movie stars, NFL quarterbacks, Mafia hit men, Ku Klux Klansmen, skid-row drunks, Middle Eastern terrorists, captains of Industry, union leaders, professional deadbeats, illegal migrant workers, destitute welfare mothers, ordinary moms and pops, and criminals of every description. Most of these interview subjects had something to hide. My job was to ferret out their secrets to support TV news reports or courtroom litigation. I quickly learned that even the most cautious people will say damning things when skillfully questioned by a prepared and professional interviewer.

I learned how to do investigative interviews the hard way—through daily practice and lots of trial and error in newsrooms and on the streets, under the mentoring of tough-nosed editors and hard-boiled private eyes. I wish *The Art of Investigative Interviewing* had been available when I started my career, because it would have prevented many errors and humiliating embarrassments I experienced along the way. Believe me, there's nothing like bungling an interview on live TV to cut you down to size in a hurry!

I heartily recommend this book to both the novice and veteran interviewer. With the proliferation of pop psychology fads in our media and colleges, it is remarkably difficult to find solid information on interviewing techniques that is both time-tested and reliable. The information revealed in *The Art of Investigative Interviewing* is worth its weight in gold, and no successful investigator can ever afford to stop learning.

I have learned repeatedly throughout my career that every investigation is only as good as the information it gathers and you can never ignore the human factor. Though an enormous number of facts can be determined through examination of written records and physical evidence, the information from human sources is always of critical importance to provide us with the full truth of events. Interviewing is a form of communication and evidence-gathering. Getting accurate and truthful information out of people is always a challenge, even for the most highly trained investigative interviewer.

This book will help you learn how to develop and discover the human intelligence information that solves cases. Furthermore, learning investigative interviewing skills will help you in all aspects of your personal and professional life, because the techniques will help you distinguish fact from fiction and give you a competitive edge over others.

The job of an investigative interviewer is tough under the best of circumstances. The mission is to have a structured conversation that elicits information useful to establishing facts and determining culpability from interview subjects who are often evasive, reluctant, or hostile. It is an art to persuade any person to let us into his or her mind at the critical moments of an event so that we can get an insider's view of the action. The best investigative interviewers allow the person to talk about himself and describe a situation step by step from his own perspective and to talk about how he overcame obstacles along the way, all while guiding him into disclosing significant facts or admitting culpability he would otherwise conceal.

In my experience, a good investigative interview yields information that can be divided into "hard" and "soft" categories. Hard information stated in an interview consists of the simple facts that often can be independently corroborated to help build a case. But interviews that generate only those facts usually lack richness and depth.

Often more important is the "soft information" of human experience revealed during an interview, the complex tapestry of personal dramas, emotions, intentions, thoughts, reactions, values, and degrees of commitment or determination. It is the soft information that helps us establish motive and develops the color that provides us with a truer understanding of any event or situation. In trying to ascertain fact, there is no substitute for observing human behavior.

There is an old Chinese adage that a picture is worth a thousand words. That is true. But I learned in TV news that a videotape is worth a million words when it shows the body language of a smirk or arched eyebrow, the physical and verbal gyrations of an agonized confession, a vocal tone of arrogance or sarcasm, or the hysterical sobbing of an interviewee repenting their criminal deeds. There is no substitute for an effective investigative interview of a human being.

Many years ago, I investigated a powerful politician who was lining his pockets with graft and was introducing legislation that benefited his hidden personal financial interests. The documents I collected laid out the facts in great detail. But it was the TV investigative interview, in which the politician nonchalantly and flippantly admitted his misconduct without any visible remorse, that told the full story and gave it life. His political career fizzled quickly after the TV audience saw and heard his performance.

So what are the traits of truly great investigative interviewers? They have constant curiosity and an unquenchable thirst for knowledge. They prepare for an interview by researching in advance as much information as possible. They know what the answers to questions are likely to be before they are asked. They know that asking obviously well-informed questions helps create a sense of intimacy and often throws the people being questioned off balance by signaling that the interviewer is not to be taken lightly. They know how to quickly establish rapport and personal chemistry with the interview subject, then ask a blend of both open-ended and pointed questions with impeccable and precise timing while carefully listening to the responses to achieve successful results. They are excellent listeners of the spoken word and observers of unspoken body language. They can be simultaneously both gentle and tough questioners. They have a taste for going for the jugular while instinctively knowing when to back off or shift gears if the interview takes unexpected and useful turns. And they know how to keep their own emotions in check while hearing the most graphic and disturbing revelations.

Investigative interviewers usually make their biggest mistakes when they become impatient and try to speed up interviews to get key information. A skilled interviewer understands the value in taking plenty of time to listen and elicit information. Speeding up the process usually creates more problems than it solves, especially when interview subjects lose their comfort zone and begin to evade or clam up.

Skilled interviewers also know when to ask a pointed question and then shut up. Staying silent often causes an interview subject to fill in the uncomfortable gap by carrying on the conversation and inadvertently disclosing valuable information. Most people need some time to grapple with their thoughts and develop a response. Often a gem pops out of the interview subject's mouth just because the questioner was silent.

The best interviewers always invite the last word from those being questioned. They ask whether there is anything else that should be discussed or if there is any question the other person would like to ask. Sometimes an unexplored angle reveals the most useful information. These techniques and much more are explained in depth in *The Art of Investigative Interviewing*.

Investigative interviewing skills are not easy to acquire. It takes years of practice and experience to perfect them. As a veteran investigative journalist and private investigator, I say without reservation that this book will help you. Study it carefully and keep it handy for future reference. I am confident that the knowledge gained from studying *The Art of Investigative Interviewing* will greatly help shorten the learning curve for you to become a master of the art.

Good luck in your continuing search for truth and justice.

Pat Clawson
Private investigator former investigative reporter for CNN
and NBC News, Flint, Michigan, and Washington, DC

INTRODUCTION

When I was approached to write this third edition of *The Art of Investigative Interviewing*, it seemed more than a coincidence. Charles Yeschke, author of the first and second editions, had been a friend and mentor to me for over 25 years. For many years Chuck and I were both involved members in the Minnesota Chapter of the American Society for Industrial Security (ASIS) International. In my young career, I had attended one of Chuck's classes on interviewing, and he autographed his first edition of this book for me. Chuck went on the write the second edition. I felt honored and privileged to be asked to write this, the third edition, because of the connection I had to both Chuck and to the subject matter. The title, *The Art of Investigative Interviewing*, is so significant and relevant because interviewing is indeed an *art*. When I started my career in security management after studying both law enforcement and criminal justice, most of my peers and definitely most of my predecessors had came from either a military background or a law enforcement background. The interviewing techniques used through the 1980s, which incorporated coercion and confrontation, are definitely different from the communication techniques used in 2013. Investigators in the corporate and private sector did not have to use the *Miranda* warning (since 1966 it had become the practice of police investigators to read suspects their rights before questioning). Over the years I trained in both the Reid technique of interviewing as well as the Wicklander-Zulawski approach. Over years of experience and training, skilled interviewers fine-tune their skills, along with honing their personal styles, to become successful interviewers.

My philosophy is to approach each interview with the knowledge that there is a high probability that you may only get one chance to interview your subject and to be fully prepared so that it can be successful in giving you whatever information you are searching for.

My goal in writing this book is to pass some of the skills I have learned through the years onto new interviewers or those who only rarely conduct interviews but who need the information as much as skilled interviewers do. Interviewers have to draw on elements from psychology, philosophy, and sociology as well as from their own personal empathy, respect, and compassion. We discuss all these elements throughout the book, along with the importance of preparation and determining the goal of each interview.

We also discuss other factors that should be considered, such as the setting, location, and intensity of the interview.

Each interviewer brings unique skills to the task because of his or her personality and experience. Interviewing is indeed an art because each of us is unique in how we conduct interviews.

Inge Sebyan Black

CHAPTER 1

So You Want to Be an Investigative Interviewer?

INTERVIEWING, INTERROGATIONS, AND INVESTIGATIONS

There are hundreds of books on interviewing, interrogations, and investigations for law enforcement, but if you are in the private sector or work for a corporation, there are differences. Those differences can often work in your favor. This book is written for those of you who will conduct interviews outside of a law enforcement environment. The one big difference in the United States is that if you are in the private sector, you are not required to read the Miranda warning before questioning a suspect. We also have no time restrictions when talking to employees about company business. We also have access to employees' company computers, company cell phones, or any other equipment that is owned by the company, *without* a search warrant.

In the chapter ahead, we discuss the Miranda warning questions and answers, interviewing techniques, deception, and evidence. In this chapter we examine what it takes to be an investigative interviewer and some helpful tips for when the time comes to conduct that first interview. You might not be a private investigator; you could be a human resource specialist, asset protection associate, insurance investigator, loss prevention officer, security director, or owner of a business. If you take away anything from this book, the author hopes it will be an understanding of the importance of preparing for an interview and how in these times, research is infinite and critical to a successful interview. That first interview might be the only chance you'll ever have to talk to your interviewee. As a private investigator, one shot may be all you'll get.

Investigative interviewing is definitely an art. It is an art because no two people are the same, which translates into every interviewer having unique mannerisms and techniques. Each will bring to the process different components, including personalities, traits, and styles. Individual style will be determined by the interviewer's work experience, personal life experience, and training. There are as many variables as there are individuals. No one can tell you what to do, what to ask, or what to say. What I *can* tell you is that with training and practice, you can be a successful interviewer. Through practice, you can perfect your individual style. All of the suggestions and descriptions in this book are just that—suggestions. They represent one or two individual styles, but not yours. Your style is unique to you.

In this first chapter we discuss some tools that I have personally found to be useful. You may also find some of these useful, or maybe they won't apply to the interviews you conduct, or maybe they simply don't work with your personality. In Chapter 6 we discuss differences between public and private interviewing, and in Chapter 11 we look at questioning techniques.

BENEFITS OF BEING A NOTARY PUBLIC

One investigative interviewing tool is obtaining authorization as a notary. Depending on the country you live or work in, this might not be possible. In Canada, being a notary varies among provinces and territories and the process can take years. For example, in Quebec and Manitoba, only individuals with law degrees can apply to be notaries. In British Columbia, an applicant only has to have taken a university course. In Ontario, they allow both lawyer and nonlawyer notaries public, but if you are not a lawyer, there is a three-year term appointment and application is through the attorney general's office. In the United States, a notary public is someone appointed by a state government. In 32 states, the main requirement is to fill out a form and pay a fee, whereas other states have restrictions on applicants with criminal histories. In 18 states, applicants have to take a course, pass an exam, or both. These are just a few examples of how becoming a notary will vary by locale.

Being able to interview a subject, take a statement, and notarize it eliminates the consequences of what could happen if the interviewee refuses to meet with you again. Being a notary ensures that the interviewee's statement and signature are captured the first time. You also do not need to be concerned about having a witness who is also a notary with you. Meeting and interviewing someone that first time might very well be the last time. If you are with a law enforcement agency, you will likely find it easier to see and interview someone multiple times, but in the private sector this is not always the case. In many interviews I have done as a private investigator, once I finished and have left the interviewee, something happened. That something was that the interviewee suddenly realized that the information he gave me might affect a relationship, a job, or his family or might affect the interviewee himself in another way. Interviewees will likely realize that they should *not* have talked to you. They have second thoughts, and when you go back to have them sign the statement, they suddenly can't remember that they said anything and refuse to sign the document.

The case that led to my becoming a notary was a sexual harassment and assault case that I worked on for my client, the lawyer representing the victim. The key witness, who could substantiate the victim's story, agreed to talk with me and provided information that would prove the victim's story. The witness opened up and gave pertinent details of what he knew and saw. I was not a notary at this time (in 1994). I returned to the corporate office of the business involved, and the witness refused to sign or notarize the statement he'd made. He stated that after he spoke to me the first time, he realized that since he still worked at the company, he couldn't risk his job by giving such a statement and refused to meet with me again. Of course, this adversely affected the victim's case, and we had to look at alternatives to help support and win the case. This is when being a notary is invaluable.

As a notary, you interview, obtain answers pertinent to the case, and write (in complete, clear, detailed sentences) the described facts as they were told to you, read the statement to the interviewee, and verbally verify what they told you. If the statement is correct, the interviewee needs to sign and date the document, at which time you will notarize it. I can't tell you the number of cases that I successfully concluded because of the handwritten, notarized statement. Another case involved three individuals who had assaulted another individual and had bribed and threatened approximately six witnesses. I interviewed all the witnesses, who eventually lied on the stand in court. However, I had taken all of their statements by hand and notarized them, and the case was won based on these statements. Since this case, I am always prepared for the reality that I may have just one shot at interviewing someone. Assuming that you might have only one interview with your subject will force you to be fully prepared when you conduct your research, plan your questions, set the timing and setting, and finally, get the interview.

Another tool that may be available to you, depending on local and state laws, is to tape record your interview. You will have to examine the laws in your state. In Minnesota, only one party needs to know that the conversation is being taped. In some states, all parties must be advised. I have often taped interviews, not necessarily because I needed recordings or was required by my client to do so, but if the interviewee later disputes in court what they said, the interviewee has committed perjury. When you are alone interviewing, this technique may help protect your integrity. Your client may or may not want to be advised of your intent to record interviews. I suggest you research your local and state laws and discuss this possibility with your client when you initially take a case and prior to taping the interview. My experience is that attorneys have not always agreed with this practice. The other benefit of tape recording interviews is that you don't have to worry about taking notes continuously, which means that you can concentrate on being an active listener. Recording interviews may also assist you in analyzing them for signs of deception.

RESEARCH TOOLS

Research is an extremely significant tool in the current Internet era. Never underestimate what research can do for your interview. Every investigator has favorite Websites and ways to research. This is a technique you will develop over time. I prefer to run a background check on my interviewee using TLOxp, an online investigative system that provides public and private records, helps with identity authentication, aids in fraud prevention and detection, and analyzes millions of records at a time. I rely on this as my first step; it allows me to look over individual assets and records to help me determine what else I would like to research or spend time on. This is only one example of a tool that some investigators use. The ones you choose will likely depend on what your client uses or has access to. Some firms already have license agreements with an investigative system. It may also depend on whether you have the necessary licenses and background for a particular company. Some require their clients to be attorneys, licensed investigators, reporters, or law enforcement. They may also require you to reside in a particular country. You will have to do some research to determine what company will serve your needs best, along with your qualifications to access the company's database. Tools such as TLOxp are governed by the Gramm-Leach-Bliley (GLB) Act and the Driver's Privacy Protection Act (DPPA) and cannot be used for Federal Fair Credit Reporting Act (FCRA) purposes. FCRA prohibits purposes related to credit, insurance, employment, or other financial information.

There are many Internet tools that investigators use. Here are a few:
- Zaba Search is a free people-finder Website. A private investigator can search for public information using an individual's basic information.
- Internet Achieve is a site that provides historical data on thousands of books, sites, moving images, and even federal court cases.

- E-investigator is a comprehensive site that provides a multitude of resources for private investigators.
- Criminal Searches is a website that provides criminal histories on people.
- Some specific sites to search mobile phones, car history, employment history, investigator tools, or people search tools are:
  - www.mobilephoneno.com
  - www.carfax.com/entry.cfx
  - www.theworknumber.com
  - www.pimall.com
  - http://find.intelius.com/index.php

It would take an entire book to list all the available Websites that can be useful to an investigator. Social networking sites are also very helpful in preparing for interviews. Information on these sites can help you determine deception, formulate questions, or determine background of a subject.

The most valuable tool is to develop your personal style and rapport—developing the ability to form a relationship, almost an intimate one, with your subject. This might not be necessary for witnesses or all interviewees, but if you are interviewing a subject that you need a confession from, you will need to form a close, almost intimate relationship. Doing so will require you to be empathetic without being judgmental or accusatory. You need that person to open up to you.

In conducting internal investigations, there are as many different approaches as there are investigators. One approach that I often use and that has helped me prosecute many suspect employees is to tell them I'm interviewing them about specific losses the company has had and to request their help to resolve the discrepancies. By "employing the employee" to help you, you give them a feeling of lending assistance that often disarms them and allows them to focus on resolving the losses versus the consequences that may occur because of their confessions.

PRETEXTING

Another tool that's often used by investigators is *pretexting*. Pretexting, otherwise known as a false motive or façade, is a social engineering tool involving someone lying to obtain information. Using pretexting can be seen as sneaking and as a cover-up to gain information. The information may be privileged, but it's not always—just as obtaining it through pretexting is sometimes illegal, but not always. Pretexting may be pretending to be someone you're not and can be used to confirm the identity of a person the investigator is talking to or to gather information, location, or data about another person. An investigator may pose as an authority figure (a law enforcement agent) or use a story, usually involving money due the potential subject, to get the location, phone numbers, or employment of that subject.

In 1999, the Gramm–Leach–Bliley (GLB) Act banned the use of pretexting to gain financial data on individuals. The GLB Act specifically addresses pretexting as an illegal act but only specifically addresses pretexting as it pertains to financial information. The GLB Act applies to all organizations that handle financial data, including credit unions, tax preparers, banks, collection agencies, credit-reporting agencies, and real estate firms. The act does not apply to information that is on public record, such as bankruptcy, police records, real estate transactions, and property taxes. The distinction between whether a particular pretexting is legal or illegal is blurred with regard to telephone, cell phone, texting, email, or any other telecommunications records, since the laws regulating privacy from information gathering vary from state to state. Often investigators use pretexting to find a particular subject that they need to interview, or it may be used to determine a timeframe in which to conduct an interview. The more important discussion to have about pretexting is professional responsibility.

In Chapter 2 we discuss ethics and professionalism and draw discussions around the concepts of right and wrong or ethical and unethical behavior and practices. Ethical issues were raised by the Hewlett-Packard (HP) Board of Directors members' use of pretexting in 2010, during the investigation of corporate information leaks. This case was about the HP Board hiring a private investigator to determine who was leaking confidential information to the press. HP's choice to use pretexting included egocentrism and pressure to produce results. These are never valid reasons to conduct unethical or illegal practices. This issue is an ethical concern. Ultimately the use of pretexting was ruled to be a nonissue and not illegal; however, this in itself does not mean that it was a good business decision. The fallout that came from this activity had negative repercussions for many members of the board; some resigned and had their professional reputations questioned. The use of pretexting elicited debate over the legality and ethicality of pretexting. Private investigators need to know that if they engage in deception, otherwise known as pretexting, the Federal Trade Commission (FTC) can become involved. The FTC, mandated by Congress, has the obligation and authority to ensure that individuals are not subject to any deceptive business practices, including pretexting on the part of investigators.

QUALIFICATIONS PREFERRED

Investigators need as much training, qualifications, and practice that is possible to work particular cases. There are investigators that specialize in the areas of fraud, arson, and auto theft as well as background investigators and insurance investigators, just to name a few areas of specialization. Generally speaking, investigators will find the following qualifications in demand by employers:

- Communication skills, both written and verbal
- Intelligence—the ability to see the entire picture; not stuck in tunnel vision; insightfulness
- Persistence—having drive; how badly to you want to know the truth, and will you put in the work?
- Training—have you had training and in what specific areas?
- Perseverance
- Patience—needed because time is necessary to uncover the truth and get the results you want
- Attention to detail—even to the slightest bits of evidence or items that may be overlooked; thoroughness
- Curiosity—a need to know
- Sensitivity—empathy; respect for yourself and others
- Ethical—being honest and having the courage to uncover truth despite obstacles

You might have to conduct an interview, or you may decide that becoming an investigative interviewer is something you want to pursue. If that is the case, remember to practice, practice and practice some more.

CHAPTER 2

Ethical Standards and Professionalism

ETHICAL STANDARDS

It seems appropriate that ethics is one of the first subjects we discuss in this book. For a certified fraud examiner, ethics training is required annually. Many positions involving interviewing, investigating, security, fraud, and compliance also require such training. There are reasons that annual ethics training is mandated and why it is critical. In this chapter we discuss the way that ethics defines our professionalism as investigative interviewers and why we need to understand and work within a set of ethical principles.

There is no universal code for private investigators; therefore, guidelines are set up by various professional departments, organizations, or industries. Furthermore, regulatory agencies around the globe have developed a code of ethics and guidelines for practicing investigators. These codes of ethics are established to promote and inspire confidence in our profession. *Truth, fairness,* and *honesty* are just some of the words we use when talking about ethics and principles.

It is essential, vital, and necessary to have ethical standards in our profession because potential consequences of interrogations are so great. If we want to be seen as a professional in the investigations industry, we need to maintain a set of principles. Ethics is something we hear about or talk about, but not everyone truly understands their ethical responsibility and the role ethics plays for those of us who conduct interviews.

Ethics is about human relationships and how we conduct ourselves, both in private and in groups. How and when are we taught about ethics? No matter whom we are interviewing or what the offense we are investigating, we must adhere to ethical standards. There is no absolute rule defining what is or is not ethical. In interviewing, your conscience will act as your guide to ethical behavior. Following ethical standards is inherently about right and wrong.

Ethics is the inherent inner voice, the source of self-control in the absence of external compulsion. Ethics can be defined as the difference between knowing the right thing to do and knowing what you have a right to do. Ethics can be said to be based on the Golden Rule: "Do unto others as you would have them do unto you." Ethical behavior is judged by the way we act, the values that motivate us, the policies we have adopted, and the goals we seek to achieve. Every organization has an ethics strategy, whether explicit or implied. Each organization needs to have its specific ethical standards written down, describing its strategy. The organization will want to implement goals based on what it wants to achieve. In the absence of policy, procedures, or precedents, ethical effectiveness is based on organizational values that provide direction and consistency in decision making.

The definition often used to describe ethics is *moral principles* or *a system of moral principles*. Although the words *ethics* and *morals* may be quite different, depending on a particular class, group, or culture, they are both about values relating to human conduct with respect to right or wrong. Ethics may be defined individually, but as a professional, ethical behavior should be seen as vital. We all respond to moral dilemmas differently because we all have fundamental differences in our personal values. Ethics rely on personality traits such as values and attitude.

For an interviewer, the line between ethical interview techniques and coercion can be a very fine one. We often look to others for moral guidance if we are in an unfamiliar situation. Ethics that are realistic and worth supporting are situational ethics; what is occurring at any given point determines what actions are effective, appropriate, and ethical.

- Values define who you are. All ethical decisions are determined by values that are clear and uncompromising statements about what is critically important. In organizations, clear values drive mission statements, strategic plans, and effective, results-oriented behavior.
- Ethics come into play when external pressures push someone to act in a manner that is not consistent with his or her values. Only actions can be judged to be ethical or unethical. Ethics do not define what is acceptable about an action as much as they define what is *not* acceptable.
- Ethics provide guidelines that outline what constitutes appropriate behavior. Once a clearly stated code of ethics is developed and made public, individuals are responsible for their own actions. The code of ethics supports the concept of dignity as the central element that drives human interaction in the workplace. Most organizational codes of ethics clearly demand that people treat each other with respect. When we show consideration for others, we are indicating that we hold them in high regard.
- A code of ethics provides a commonly held set of guidelines that will provide a consistent, value-driven basis for judging what is right or

wrong in any given situation and establishes the outer limits of acceptable behavior.

• If a new code of ethics is going to be truly operational, people must have an opportunity to see where the ethics originate, what purpose they serve, and how they relate to each individual.

One might say ethics involve doing the right thing when no one is looking. Having a code of ethics will guide you as an interviewer to be respectful, honest, and reputable in your actions because the impact of your behavior can involve life-changing consequences.

ETHICS FROM THE TOP DOWN

It is essential to have ethical leadership in any organization. Employees of organizations look to their leaders for ethical guidance and moral development. Ethical leadership can be very complex, and it goes much deeper than simply having strong morals or good character. An organization having ethical leadership sends a clear message about its ethics and values. This type of leadership also holds employees responsible and accountable for living up to these standards. This type of leadership makes the effort to find and develop the best people. To find the right people, consideration for ethics and character come into the selection and hiring process. Ethical leaders send the message that the organization has an ethical line and will reward good behavior and act decisively when moral and ethical lapses occur. These leaders have a deep sense of ethical principles, values, and character at the center of their leadership. These strengths are reinforced through training and communication.

Conversations about ethics should routinely occur across all levels of business so that people can hold each other responsible and accountable. All employees should share in the responsibility for creating and maintaining an ethical culture. To accomplish this goal, leaders need to have a live conversation about whether they are living the values and bringing respect and compassion to their management of people. Leaders at the highest levels of organization must clearly demonstrate their commitment to ethical behavior through their words and actions. Ethical leadership can be and should be incorporated into development programs for management. We all can be ethical leaders by looking at and reviewing our own behavior and values. We also need to make a commitment to accept responsibility for the effects of our actions on others and ourselves.

It is also essential to have a written code of conduct that clearly states what is and what is not acceptable. This code of conduct must be created from the bottom up, with input from employees at all levels. Ethical leaders need to put resources in place to let employees know what will and will not be tolerated and that if an incident occurs, the organization will take strong action. There also needs to be a process in place for reporting any corrupt or unethical activities.

THE CODE OF ETHICS

Having a code of ethics helps guide us in decision making. Being professional means more than this, but it is a necessary requirement.

Whether you conduct interviews for the government, the public sector, the private sector, or a corporation, it is likely that you will be guided by some form of a code of ethics. Common elements within a code of ethics are as follows:

- Work in accordance to any local, state, provincial, or government laws
- Work within company policies, if this applies
- Be honest and impartial
- Remain objective
- Maintain the highest standard of morals and ethics
- Have and maintain integrity
- Provide truthful and accurate reports
- Respect the inherent dignity of all people
- Be diligent
- Be ethical in soliciting business
- Never disclose confidential information
- Never knowingly cause harm
- Accept no illegal or improper remuneration for services rendered
- Refrain from representing competing or conflicting interests or the perception of conflicting interests
- Support the purposes and objectives of the profession
- Refrain from negative comment about other interviewers

While researching ethics for investigators and security professionals, I found out that there are many ethics codes. Some countries have their ethical standards, some states have their own, and then there are professional organizations that have theirs. One particular ethical and behavioral standard that I felt was relevant and specifically addresses professional conduct of security professionals as well as investigators is described in the following section.

As a matter of fact, this code was endorsed in the spring of 2013 by the Australasian Council of Security Professionals and provided to me by my co-council on the 2013 ASIS Crime Prevention/Loss Prevention Council, Ray Andersson.

Ethics and Behavioral Standards[1]

The Australasian Council of Security Professionals has created a code of conduct for the Security Profession:

> *All security professionals and organizations must operate to the highest ethical values to engender trust in all those they encounter in a professional capacity.*
>
> *Given the security industry's high profile, this Code of Ethical Conduct sets a standard that security professionals shall adhere to in their working habits and professional relationships. The values on which it is based apply to all situations in which Security Professionals participate and exercise their judgment.*
>
> *Registered security professionals are required to comply with the Code in all of their professional activities. Failure to do so may be referred to the Security Professionals Registry – Australasia for disciplinary action.*

Security Professionals' Code of Conduct

The ASCP Code of Ethical Conduct requires that a security professional must operate to the highest ethical standards with all those they encounter in a professional capacity and shall:

1. *Act in the interests of the security of society and their client.* A security professional shall:
    a. Act honorably, responsibly, diligently, and lawfully and uphold the reputation, standing, and dignity of the Security Profession within society.
    b. Not act recklessly, maliciously, or in a manner that will negatively impact the reputation of other individuals or organizations.
    c. Act in the interests of the security of society and their client.
    d. Act honorably, responsibly, diligently, and lawfully and uphold the reputation, standing, and dignity of the company, employer, or client to which the security professional has a professional or legal association.
2. *Perform their duties in accordance with the law at all times.* A security profession shall:

---

[1] Developed by Raymond Andersson, GAICD, AFAIM, RSecP, ICPS for the Australasian Council of Security Professionals (ASCP).

a. Act in accordance with the laws of the jurisdiction(s) in which they are performing professional services.

b. Hold paramount the health, safety, and security of others.

3. *Act and behave at all times with integrity.* A security professional shall:

a. Not abuse a professional position for personal gain and reject improper inducement.

b. Avoid conflicts of interest.

c. Avoid deceptive acts by actively taking steps to prevent corrupt practices or professional misconduct.

4. *Be diligent and competent in discharging their professional responsibilities.* A security professional shall:

a. Act for their employer or client in a reliable and trustworthy manner.

b. Never knowingly mislead or allow others to be misled.

c. Maintain currency in their security competencies through continued education and private research.

5. *Protect confidential information gained in the course of their professional activities and not disclose it to any unauthorized party nor use it for personal gain.* A security professional shall:

a. Protect client information in accordance with client information security policy.

b. Apply effective physical, procedural, and IT controls to protect client or employer information in their care from unauthorized release.

c. Implement and follow processes for the clearance of partners, employees, contractors, and other stakeholders in accordance with the classification of accessed client or employer information.

d. Apply the need-to-know principle.

6. *Not maliciously damage the professional reputation or practice of colleagues, clients, or employers.* A security professional shall:

a. Refrain from unfounded criticism of work carried out by Security Professionals.

b. Refrain from action deliberately designed to damage a colleague, client, or employer.

7. *Not knowingly undertake any action that brings the profession into disrepute.* A Security Professional shall:

a. Be objective and truthful in any statement made in their professional capacity.

b. Act honorably, responsibly, diligently, and lawfully and uphold the reputation, standing, and dignity of the profession.

   c.   Not engage in acts of collusion, corruption, or breaches of the law.

   d.   Be a positive role model for others in the profession.[2]

ETHICAL AND UNETHICAL INTERVIEWING

Throughout recorded history, one of the great problems we have faced has been the development of a system by which truth may be made known. Solutions to this problem have ranged from such extremes as the torture chambers of the Middle Ages to the unhesitating acceptance of the word of a gentleman in the 18th century. Neither extreme meets the requirements of today. We respect human dignity too much to permit physical and psychological abuse of an individual in the search for truth. Yet we recognize that many individuals will lie without hesitation, even under oath, if this will further their aims. The truth can be determined only after the evidence has been collected and analyzed. The public should not be misled into thinking that this is an automatic process. Investigative interviewers should use only the most ethical means available on behalf of society to obtain statements and the truth.

There has been a critical analysis of various types of interview training in North America. Through the course of this analysis, new regulations have been formulated. Due to miscarriages of justice in some leading cases across the country, increased training of interviewers has occurred. Although each country has its own training programs, many programs have common features. The emphasis of an interview should also be on the search for the truth and on the collection of reliable information and, ultimately, a higher quality of information.

The interviewing tactics suggested in this book to encourage the cooperation of interviewees are ethical, as defined in this chapter. This book is partly intended to counteract the often illegal coercive tactics of the past and to promote perceptive interviewing. The following behaviors are considered unethical in North America but sadly are still used throughout the world:

- Using interrogation tactics instead of interviewing tactics
- Treating each interviewee as though culpable, with little or no regard for the destructive public relations and psychological damage inflicted on interviewees who are blameless
- Making threats

[2] The Australasian Council of Security Professionals (ACSP).

- Making illegal promises
- Using coercion
- Using duress
- Using force or the threat of force
- Employing ruthless methods
- Falsely imprisoning the interviewee
- Not respecting the interviewee
- Not maintaining the interviewee's dignity

These and similar tactics have been used in the past in interviews with victims and witnesses as well as suspects. It is time for change. It is time that those involved in investigative interviewing be specifically taught what is ethical and what is unethical, beyond what is legal and what is illegal.

CONFLICTS OF INTEREST

As a professional, we must not engage in activities that may involve or create the perception of a conflict of interest. *Conflict of interest* can be defined as a situation in which one's external interests undermine or appear to undermine the investigators' ability to perform their legal, ethical, or professional duties. Conflict of interest might impair the investigators' judgment or create the impression that it does. Organizational conflict can be as complicated as personal conflict. We should always remain free of any interest or relationship that is connected to our clients.

There are many questions that you can ask yourself to avoid a conflict of interest:

- Do you have a personal relationship with the person you will be interviewing or another person who has an interest in the case?
- Do you have any financial relationship with the person you will be interviewing?
- Is this case somehow related to another organization you are working with?
- Do you have a professional relationship to another person or organization that is associated in any way to the case you are working on?
- Do you have any personal or professional bias that would make others question your ability to handle this case fairly and ethically?
- Would you personally benefit in any way from conducting interviews for this case?
- Have you had any direct knowledge of policies or practices that would affect the interviews you are about to do?
- Have you already formed an opinion on this case?

REVIEW QUESTIONS

1. Why are ethical standard so critical for investigative interviewers?
2. Who is responsible for developing a code of ethics?
3. Is there one universal code of ethics for those who conduct interviews?
4. What is the Golden Rule and how does it apply to ethics?
5. How do we learn our personal values?
6. Who is responsible for clearly defining ethical behavior in an organization?
7. Why should organizations have a written code of conduct?
8. List three ethical guidelines that might appear in a code of ethics.
9. List three interviewing tactics that you believe are unethical and explain why.

CHAPTER 3

Preparation and So Much More

PREPARATION

Investigative interviewing is about having a conversation that results in information. This information, or fact-finding, is your goal. Successfully reaching your goal will result in solving your case. You might think that success comes only from a confession, but there is so much more that comes from fruitful conversations. Having a conversation might sound easy, but as an investigator or interviewer you must be *prepared* for this conversation. Preparation is the single most important aspect of a successful interview. Even if you have a natural ability to interview, you still have to prepare. Preparation involves attitude, psychology, intuition, flexibility, curiosity, imagination, and research. This chapter takes you through each of these factors, the role each plays in every interview, and how you can use them successfully.

ATTITUDE

Why do we talk about attitude if we are interviewing a suspect, witness, or victim? If you want information from an interviewee, you need to know what attitude you should have with that person in order to obtain the response or information that you are seeking.

If the response you seek in an interview is full and open cooperation, you must maintain a positive attitude toward each and every interviewee. Each of us has a history filled with experience, which creates bias and prejudices. That experience will determine the preconceived opinions and perceptions with which we go into each interview. I encourage you to be honest with yourself and understand how and why you have formed your specific opinions, so that you can conduct each interview in a fair and impartial way, treating each interviewee with a level of respect. In addition, understand how your discriminatory actions affect others.

Showing respect means remaining calm, actively listening, and maintaining a positive attitude. By having confidence in your skills and ability, you will display that you are self-assured. Neighborliness will sow positive seeds of your attitude, persistence, and general determination along the investigative path. Sensing your helping, friendly attitude, interviewees will probably comply as expected. A positive attitude is always effective, no matter what your objective.

Perceptive interviewees can sense your attitude as it is expressed through the formulation and presentation of your questions and by the way you listen to the responses. They are keenly aware of verbal and nonverbal signals expressing negative attitudes. If you ridicule or degrade interviewees, you will only promote antagonism.

Characteristics of a positive attitude are warmth, empathy, acceptance, caring, and respect. You should learn to have and project these qualities because they will help you become a proficient interviewer.

These are three important qualities to incorporate into your positive attitude:

- *Congruence.* To be in congruence with yourself means to be aware of and comfortable with your feelings and to be able to communicate constructively with interviewees in a way that expresses your humanity. To be in congruence with the interviewee means to recognize and accept the human qualities, needs, and goals that we all share.
- *Unconditional positive regard.* Just as a parent expresses unconditional love for a child, you should strive to display a positive regard for interviewees, without reservations or judgments. Regardless of the inquiry and even when dealing with unsavory interviewees, treat everyone as a valuable human being. Develop a genuine liking for people, and be tolerant of human weakness. When you're dealing with interviewees you consider repugnant, do not show how you really feel. When your inner feelings are critical of the interviewee's behavior, put on a convincing show of acceptance of or tolerance for their behavior. This show is intended to encourage interviewees to let down their guard when talking with you. As I said earlier, identifying your prejudices and biases will help you understand the people you interview and avoid prejudging them.
- *Empathy.* Empathy is the ability to identify with someone else, to understand their thoughts and feelings from their perspective. Pay attention as interviewees express themselves verbally and nonverbally so that you can pick up on their messages. Interviewees often express some deep emotional hurt that influenced their behavior in some way. By comprehending those hurts and putting them into your own words, you show that you are deeply tuned in, and this expresses closeness and caring.

Controlling your negative feelings throughout an investigation and with interviewees will be invaluable. Avoid being condescending or patronizing. These feelings will only cause antagonist behavior. Keep in mind, your goal is to get information that will help solve a case. Obtaining the facts and not being judgmental will affect the outcome. If you have negative feelings, you can change them if you really desire to change. As a professional, you can make a commitment to modify your attitudes and thus change your behavior to become a more effective interviewer. To change your attitudes, you must first change your feelings or your thinking. Authoritarianism, which breeds resentment, retaliation, and reluctance or refusal to cooperate, is based on your biases and prejudices.

A significant challenge is to become aware of your own strengths and limitations. The more aware you are of your good and bad qualities as an investigator, the more likely it is that you will make changes to improve yourself. Having a positive attitude is the first important step you will take to prepare for interviews.

PSYCHOLOGY

Psychology plays an integral role in an interview. We need to prepare psychologically for each interview, and we need to understand psychology to help interpret and assess the interview as the interviewee speaks and reacts.

Let's start by talking about how to prepare psychologically. We discussed attitude in the previous section; part of our attitude is to enter the interview with an open mind. We also discussed being accepting and nonjudgmental, even when we are interacting with people we consider suspects. We have to understand the psychology of human needs and understand how remaining positive will go a long way toward achieving our success.

The effective interviewer sets the stage for eliciting accurate information by knowing, accepting, and attempting to satisfy the emotional needs that motivate all human activity. We have to be aware of the subliminal messages we are sending as well the ones we are receiving. As stated earlier, communication is the way you get information, but communication is an extremely complex process in which psychology plays a role. We will get information only if we communicate effectively, form a rapport with the interviewee, and understand the psychology behind why the interviewee will give us information. Having knowledge of the psychology of interviewing will make you a more effective interviewer.

The fundamentals of human personality are needs, emotions, thinking, and the ability to relate thoughts and feelings. Our actions are a result and composite of all these elements. Humans function mostly on feelings and not logic. But most of all, it is the satisfaction of meeting essential and predictable needs that motivates every type of human behavior. Individuals try to satisfy their needs by maintaining physical comfort, avoiding the unsafe, attempting to gain understanding, detesting anonymity, desiring to be free from boredom, fearing the unknown, and hating disorder. Underlying each interview action is a desire to satisfy one of the basic human needs: food, water, and shelter.

INTUITION

The heart has reasons of which reason has no knowledge.

—Pascal

Imagination, knowledge, and awareness combine to produce intuition. Intuition has many other names: instinct, perception, gut feeling, hunch, sixth sense, third ear, reading between the lines, quick insight. Intuition is the power of knowing through the senses, without recourse to inference or reasoning. As Edward Sapir (1884–1939), an American anthropologist who laid the foundation for modern linguistics, wrote: "We respond to gestures with an extreme alertness and, one might say, in accordance with an elaborate code that is written nowhere, known by none, and understood by all" (Sapir, 1949, pp. 533–543). Most people possess a remarkable sensitivity to others, but their intuition remains dormant in the subconscious because it is never brought into play. The seeds of intuition are probably within you to be discovered, nurtured, and enhanced.

Although some people disregard intuition and consider its use unscholarly, I believe it is a valuable asset in interviewing. Keen intuition is spontaneous, accurate, and helpful, although difficult to explain. In an interview, allow your intuitive judgment to help you select the investigative pathways you will pursue. Let your intuition direct the interview and guide your responses. When you interact with interviewees, be alert to hints of facts and feelings revealed by a slip of the tongue, but conceal your interest. Subtle behavioral cues, words, gestures, and body language can direct you if you listen to your intuition. This is not to imply that you shouldn't plan your approach. Rather, a good balance is required. Acquiring a mental warehouse of information about human behavior is a must. As Alexander Pope so aptly said, "The proper study of mankind is man." With that study comes greater success.

Try to achieve a careful balance of the scientific and the intuitive so that you can avoid rigid procedures in your interviews. Listen to your intuition during an interview, and allow it to guide you through sensitive issues. If you don't, you will be unprepared for the spontaneous developments that occur in most interviews. As the Greek philosopher Heraclitus proclaimed around 500 B.C., "If you expect not the unexpected, ye shall not find the truth." Since seeking truth is your primary objective, you must expect the unexpected.

Trust yourself to understand what your intuition senses. Seemingly insignificant nonverbal messages may help you develop the information you need. Bodily tension, flushing, excitability, frustration, ambiguousness, depression, and sadness can either confirm or contradict the interviewee's words. Actively listen by drawing on your knowledge and your experiences stored in your subconscious. The subtleties of the interviewee's behavior can influence your judgment. Therefore, concentrate on using your intuition, knowledge, and experience to capture every subtlety you sense.

At first, you may not understand the apparently arbitrary techniques used by skilled interviewers. They frequently cannot explain the role of intuition in their interviewing process. Still, proficient interviewers confidently nurture their intuitive judgments and act on them. They sense the interviewee's tenseness and spontaneously select the words or actions that will encourage truthful responses. If you want to follow their example, you will have to learn how to trust your intuition. This will come through practice and experience. You will find that your total sensing of the situation, along with your common sense, is more trustworthy than your intellect.

In almost all worthwhile endeavors, the degree of your success is directly related to the effort you make. This applies equally to using intuition. Initially, rely on your self-confidence to implement your intuitive judgments, and be prepared to learn from your success or failure. Work through the various steps of interviewing, following the generally accepted concepts, but also work on developing techniques that capitalize on your intuitive talents. Use your intuition positively to read the interviewee's psychological movements, feelings, private logic or rationale, and any other signs that will help you achieve your goal.

The Intuition of Interviewees

Interviewees, too, are intuitive, and it would be foolhardy to ignore their ability to sense your judgments. In fact, through their exercise of their intuition, perhaps to achieve less-than-positive ends, they may have become quite skillful. Keenly alert to your signals, they respond positively or negatively to what they sense about you and your presentation. They may scrutinize your every move and gesture, the delivery of your questions, and your reactions to their answers. Therefore, ask yourself these questions:

- Have I fully researched everything possible prior to the interview?
- Do I convey a positive, self-confident, calm composure?
- Was my approach nondefensive?
- Do I keep an open mind during the interview?
- Do I demonstrate that I care about the interviewee, and am I respectful?
- Do I understand that displaying an accepting attitude toward all interviewees does not mean that I condone antisocial behavior and does not compromise my personal values?
- Do I understand that interviewees are secretly searching for a signal from me that it is indeed okay to be open and reveal the information?
- Do I consciously provide positive signals so that interviewees can count on my acceptance and fairness?
- Do I understand that I may subconsciously project my bias during interviews, triggering hostile feelings, threatening rapport, and therefore ending the interview?

FLEXIBILITY

Flexibility implies that you have the ability to change gears when and if needed in the process of interviewing. This quality is extremely important because no two interviews will ever be the same and there are no scripts for interviews. During interviewing, you need to adapt to changes in questioning, strategies, tone, or behavior.

To obtain the cooperation of some interviewees, you might need to temporarily modify your methods and thinking. You might have to do or say things that you normally find objectionable. For example, if you are neutral when interacting with the interviewee, I suggest figuratively leaning in favor of the interviewee by giving the impression that if you were in a similar circumstance, you might have done something similar to what the interviewee did, even though you know that you would never engage in that particular behavior. Treat everyone that you interview, even those you suspect of involvement in the matter under investigation, with professionalism and neutrality. Your professional, calm, nonjudgmental methods signal to victims, witnesses, and suspects that they can safely trust you.

Regardless of the style or styles of interviewing you have learned or may use, keep an open mind and stay ready to adjust your style.

Without losing sight of your objective, try several methods of questioning with uncooperative interviewees. This is where the art of interviewing enters the picture.

CURIOSITY

Curiosity or inquisitiveness is a trait that can be very helpful throughout the investigative process and during the interview process. Certainly, as investigators we are driven by wanting the answers and the truth. We are also suspicious by nature. However, questions full of genuine curiosity rather than accusatory suspicion will further your investigation.

IMAGINATION

Imagination has a part to play in training interviewers as well as in preparing for and conducting actual interviews. An excellent method for developing practical interviewing skills is to pool your ideas with one or more other imaginative interviewers. Group role playing can be used to test the ideas you generate. This approach allows less imaginative and less assertive interviewers to benefit from their more skilled peers. As general preparation for interviewing, strive to broaden your knowledge and awareness of other people in order to improve your ability to imagine the unimaginable.

Part of a successful interviewing venture is to try to consider why *you* might have done the crime in question. Imagine the motivation of the person you are interviewing while you conduct the interview. Don't be surprised by any basis for the event under investigation—people justify, blame, and rationalize in ways that sometimes lack logic.

Imagination is a special quality not shared by all investigators. Those who possess it naturally are fortunate, for it is questionable whether imagination can be taught.

RESEARCH

We can never say enough about the importance of research in preparing for an interview. Never before have we had such a powerful research tool as the Internet. The Internet has changed the way we prepare and the extent of that preparation. Before we conduct the interview, we can gather a wealth of information to prepare for everything from the interview location to the questions we ask. Thoroughly research the background of each interviewee.

It is critical to bring all important documents with you to the interview. You want to be fully prepared for whatever possibilities arise.

As a corporate and private investigator, the one critical lesson I learned early on was that I might get only one chance to interview a person. This is one particular lesson I will talk about in other chapters because I think it is worth discussing.

There are many reasons you might have only one shot at your interview, but here are a few:

- Immediately after the interview, the interviewee is remorseful as to what they just told you
- The interviewee suddenly wants to stop being cooperative.
- The interviewee is still employed at the business you are investigating and he has changed his mind as to how involved he wants to get.
- The interviewee realizes that she just said something to implicate herself.
- After the interview, someone talked to the interviewee and made him see things differently than previously stated.
- The interviewee has had a change of heart toward either the suspect or the victim.
- The interviewee has been asked not to cooperate with any investigation or with one particular side of the investigation.
- The interviewee doesn't want to commit to any investigation.

Being prepared for all of these possibilities will determine the level of success of your interview.

STYLE

Someone said once that the hardest thing about conducting an interview is the conducting of an interview. It takes practice, practice and more practice before you can develop a style.

Using psychology, attitude, intuition, and the other qualities we've discussed, you will develop your own personal style.

In preparation, consider the following questions and pointers. In the chapters ahead, these specific questions will be addressed:

- What is your purpose in conducting this interview?
- Determine whether this will be an interview or an interrogation.
- What interview techniques will you utilize?
- What qualities should you as the interviewer have to get the optimum results?
- Be confident in verbal and nonverbal indicators.

- What indicators will you use for assessing verbal behavior and evaluating nonverbal behavior?
- Are there special circumstances that need to be addressed for this interview?
- What types of questions will you use for this interview?
- In regard to the interview, know your local, state, and federal laws as well as the companies involved, if this is a corporate internal investigation.
- Where will your interview be conducted? If you are able to decide on a setting, have you prepared accordingly?

REVIEW QUESTIONS

1. How does your attitude influence the outcome of an interview?
2. Identify and discuss the three main components of a positive attitude.
3. What is the first step in changing your attitude?
4. In what ways does flexibility help during an interview?
5. Why strive to appear curious rather than suspicious?
6. What is the role of imagination in an interview?
7. What is intuition?
8. How can intuition be valuable to the interview process?
9. What role does psychology play in the interview?
10. Why should you do research before conducting the interview?

CHAPTER 4

Deception and the Interview

THE INTERVIEWER'S GOAL

Success in influencing the behavior of interviewees lies in convincing them to answer questions honestly—and that begins with your attempt to understand and, to some extent, satisfy the needs underlying their behavior. The anticipation and satisfaction of needs are central to successful interviewing. When we think of our basic, universal needs as humans, we are most often talking about security, freedom, understanding, and affection. If you fail to anticipate the interviewee's needs, tension will develop, and unless the interviewee's basic needs are fulfilled, the interview will be little more than a waste of time. Building a relationship with the person you are interviewing will determine your success. There are many skills that a seasoned investigator uses to exhibit understanding and acceptance of the interviewee's needs. By attempting to gain a deeper understanding of those needs, the investigator uncovers possible evasiveness and distress. Keep in mind that our ultimate goal is to obtain truthful statements that will ultimately lead to successful resolution of a case.

Pressures, loyalties, obligations, needs, and restrictions frequently cause interviewees to be uncomfortable and not relaxed mentally. Gaining their cooperation requires active listening, kindness, consideration, and respect. These traits are not easy to portray in many instances.

There are many different interview models, but two common ones that are used in the United States are the *Reid model*, a confrontational method, and the *Wicklander-Zulawski model*, which is a nonconfrontational method but teaches both. Both methods allow the interviewer to leverage the interviewee's physical and verbal behavior while avoiding denials in order to reach a truthful confession. Interviewers develop their own style after years of practicing, learning a variety of styles, and putting their personality into the interview.

Another interview model that is used in the United Kingdom and encouraged in Canada is known as the *PEACE model*.[1] PEACE is composed of five distinct parts:

---

[1] http://sg.jobsdb.com/investigative-interview-training-course-using-peace-model. Researched on March 17, 2013.

P: Planning and Preparation

E: Engage and explain

A: Account, clarification, and challenge

C: Closure

E: Evaluation

This came about after a number of high-profile miscarriages of justice in the United Kingdom during the 1970s and 1980s, where it was determined that the interviewing techniques used to elicit confessions were overly manipulative and employed coercion. Due to all the attention to these cases (e.g., the Guilford Four, the Birmingham Six), there was a call for close scrutiny of the police investigation process, particularly the interviewing process. In 1991, a steering group on investigative interviewing was set up, resulting in the PEACE model, now used for interviewing witnesses, victims, and suspects. The PEACE model is an inquisitorial, nonaccusatory interview model that is designed to gather information and behavioral data from an interviewee.

The Interviewer's Needs

Experienced interviewers learn to keep their own biases and feelings in check during an investigation. Investigators who try to fulfill egocentric, personal, or childish needs during an interview may become frustrated, which may lead them to act out personal tensions and misuse their authority. The potential for destructiveness goes with a position of authority. Given authority, some individuals become destructive in ways and at times that are not helpful to society or to their own goals in an investigation.

When the self-image and self-esteem of interview participants are at stake, pressure can be overwhelming. Overstimulation of the body's autonomic nervous system, which governs involuntary actions, routinely adds to distress, particularly when there is no way to vent built-up pressure. When the investigation becomes intense—stressful enough to cause emotional involvement—proficient interviewers try to remain detached.

DECEPTION

Deception and lying have many different meanings once you cross cultural borders. These cultural differences determine whether deception or some level of truth telling is acceptable. Because of these differences, it is not possible to establish a universal motive for one's deceptive behavior. Here, for the purpose of the investigative interview, we review deceptive behavior in North America and how to identify verbal and nonverbal signs of deception.

Before we explore deception, let's establish some criteria for credibility. The credibility of interviewees is based on their truthfulness and believability, and it is related to their observation skills and accuracy in reporting. Here are some possible tests of interviewee credibility:

1. Was the interviewee present and aware during the incident? Presence includes more than being there physically.
2. If questions relate to a timeline, are their statements consistent? By asking the interviewee to repeat or recall the order of events at different times during the interview, you can observe and watch for inconsistencies.
3. How well developed are the interviewee's powers of observation?
4. Can the interviewee relate the facts briefly, correctly, and clearly, without showing signs of emotional disturbance?
5. Does the interviewer's nonverbal behavior signal deception? There are some common physical signs that might indicate deception, but these same physical gestures may be stress related.

In an interview, the interviewee is deceptive when he or she makes a false statement with the intention to deceive the interviewer. Deception is generally thought to be the intentional act of concealing or distorting the truth for the purpose of misleading.

As investigators, we need to watch for inconsistencies in a story, but we also need to pay close attention to how the story is told. If the person is deceptive, there will be a variety of signals, both physically and in the words spoken. You will need to remember that the liar is also trying to read the investigator, telling her story in the way she thinks will get the best result for her. She is also trying to manage her body language, voice tone, and style. Trained investigators will have to assess all the indicators, both verbal and nonverbal.

Convincing liars are often self-assured and cunning. They can be difficult to identify because their comments are never too strong, too defensive, or out of context. Their motivation to lie is rarely based on anger or hostility; that would weaken the basis of their confidence. If they are trying to help someone by lying, they will be at ease, and their comments will sound natural. Because they have rationalized their lying, they maintain both confidence and peace of mind, suffering no question of conscience. Conscience is the internal sense of what is right and wrong that governs a person's thoughts and actions, urging him or her to do the right thing. Conscience is expressed through behavior.

Verbal Signs

Listening is one of the most important skills you will need to develop. I use the term *develop* because almost everyone can improve their listening skills. Listening is critical if you want to determine whether an interviewee is being truthful or deceptive. The interviewee might not be showing signs of stress through nonverbal signs. You will have to determine whether the information you are getting is, in fact, the truth or a lie. Sometimes the deceptive interviewee will provide too many details, or sometimes not enough.

A lack of clear thinking can signal deception and evasiveness. When interviewees express themselves in a calculated, dissociated, or awkward manner rather than in a smooth, flowing way, something, somewhere, is not altogether right. The deceptive tend to assert that they don't remember, whereas truthful interviewees tend not to say this. A person who wants to hide relevant information must make a conscious effort to keep the truth submerged. That effort requires contemplation, intention, and planning, all of which may happen in a brief moment, followed by a "memory lapse." The deceptive answer is more evasive than the truthful. The interviewee may attempt to distract the interviewer with inappropriate friendliness, compliments, or seductive behavior. They may present a complex, tangled, or confused explanation in response to your question, or they may try to dodge the question altogether. Their answers are general in nature and broad in content. Their apparent desire is to say as little as possible while hiding in their self-made emotional shelter. They may think that if they are silent and motionless, no one will guess they are hiding the truth. They seem to take comfort in their lack of spontaneity, and they think they are safe and secure as they try not to be noticed. If interviewees have to invent an answer that is a lie, they might spend more time searching for the right phrase to fit into their story.

Remember that the higher the consequences, the more pressure the person will be under.

With this kind of pressure, there are likely to be physical cues. For most people, lying is stressful, so you might try taking a break in between questions, which causes some discomfort, or changing the subject, which may cause the person to adjust or change his nonverbal cues.

When interviewees begin with the words "To be honest," "To tell the truth," "Frankly," or "Honestly," they most likely do not intend to be frank or honest. Interviewees who express objections rather than denials when questioned are probably not being completely truthful. Interviewees who were later shown to be lying have said the following:

- "I have plenty of money in the bank. I would have no reason to take that money."

- "I'm not the kind of person who would think of doing that."
- "I don't go around doing those kinds of things."
- "I couldn't do something like that."

The objections tend to be true, at least in part. The suspect who utters the first objection may indeed have money in the bank, but that response is not a clear denial of having stolen. Honest denials are straightforward and crystal clear: "No, I didn't steal the money."

After answering a question dishonestly, some interviewees immediately look searchingly at your eyes and face for any nonverbal signs of your skepticism. This subconscious, questioning, wide-open look lasts only a fraction of a moment. While deceptive interviewees pretend to ponder questions, they may engage in some physical action that betrays their desire to escape from the interview, mentally if not physically. This uneasiness may manifest itself as they shuffle their feet, cross their legs, or cover their eyes. They often avoid eye contact by looking around the room or at the floor, frequently picking real or imagined lint from their clothes. In addition, they blink more often than truthful interviewees.

Experienced investigators know that they can't rely on false clues or signs of deception such as eye behavior. Twenty-three out of 24 peer-reviewed studies published in scientific journals reporting on experiments on eye behavior as an indicator of lying have rejected this hypothesis.[2] No scientific evidence exists to suggest that eye behavior or gaze aversion can reliably gauge truthfulness. Some people say that gaze aversion is a sure sign of lying, others that fidgety feet or hands are the key indicators. Still others believe that analysis of voice stress or body posture provides benchmarks. Research has tested all of these indicators and found them only weakly associated with deception.[3]

They may appear calm, but in a forced way. Although they smile and look composed, the deceptive often seem physically restrained. Their movements are often overly controlled and repetitive, lacking complexity and variety, not spontaneous and free moving. Interviewees who engage in rehearsed gestures, without putting their bodies into motion in a smooth, convincing manner, signal their intent to deceive. They present a false image of themselves and hope that you will accept it without question.

---

[2] C. F. Bond, A. Omar, A. Mahmoud, and R. N. Bonser, "Lie Detection Across Cultures," *Journal of Nonverbal Behavior* 14 (1990): 189–204.

[3] B. M. DePaulo, J. J. Lindsay, B. E. Malone, L. Muhlenbruck, K. Charlton, and H. Cooper, "Cues to Deception," *Psychological Bulletin* 129, no. 1 (2003): 74–118.

Nonverbal Signs

Investigators can improve their ability to detect deception by becoming more aware of nonverbal cues. Gestures, mannerisms, facial expressions, and other forms of nonverbal communication are learned throughout life; they reveal underlying personality traits, subconscious attitudes, intentions, and conflicts. The more you know about nonverbal communication, the better an interviewer you will be. Your observation of the interviewee's unintentional nonverbal cues can help you make decisions about his or her truthfulness. When interviewees twist the truth, they leave clues in their facial expressions and bodily movements. Their expressions and body language may convey internal struggles as they try to cover the outward signs of lying. A mere twitch or an effort to control such a barely perceptible movement is described as a *microexpression*. Also described as a slight, unique little expression, a microexpression happens in one-fifth of a second[4]—so fast that the person can't modify or conceal it.

Microexpressions express one of the seven universal emotions,[5] which are:
- Happiness
- Surprise
- Contempt
- Sadness
- Fear
- Disgust
- Anger

Something more than a nonverbal cue indicates deception. If you look at the behavioral cues when a person is truthful and determine a baseline, you can more clearly see nonverbal cues when that person is lying. Establishing a baseline will help you observe when the person's behavior, mannerisms, and physical signs change as he moves between truthful statements and false ones. The key to detecting false statements is to look for these deviations in behavior.

Body Language and Body Physical Signs

Table 4.1 presents some potential meanings of body movements that could indicate an interviewee's state of mind.[6]

---

[4] "The Effects of the Duration of Expressions on the Recognition of Micro Expressions," *Journal of Zhejiang University*, Science B, Vol. 13, Issue 3, pp 221–230, March 1, 2012.

[5] Daniel Benjamin Smith, "Dr. Cal Lightman's Seven Universal Micro-Expressions," March 12, 2010.

[6] Louis A. Tyska, CPP, and Lawrence J. Fennelly, *Investigations: 150 Things You Should Know*, Chapter 8.

Table 4.1 The use of Micro Expressions, Body Movements vs State of Mind

Body movement	Possible meaning
Lowering the eyebrows	Concentrating or anger
Raised eyebrows	Surprise or anticipation
Widening eyes	High interest or fear
Removing glasses	Withdrawal
Closing nostrils with fingers	Contempt
Index finger alongside nose	Suspicion
Lowering chin and looking up	Coy or shy
Picking face or biting nails	Unsure, negative feelings
Fingering collar of shirt	Nervous, desire to escape
Hand over heart or middle of chest	Honesty
Playing unconsciously with ring	Possible conflict
Wiping under nose with finger	Aggression
Fingers formed in steeple shape	Superiority
Mouth falls open	Boredom or unsure of self
Flared nostrils	Aggression, critical attitude
Tongue flicking teeth	Sexually aggressive
Biting lips	Self-depreciation
Hands held behind head	Confident, superiority
Male running fingers through his hair	Uncertainty
Female playing with her hair	Flirtation
Folding hands deep in lap	Defense against rejection
Self-scratching, picking, squeezing	Aggression, hostility
Woman exposing palm to man	Flirtation
Rubbing objects	Reassurance, sensuousness
Fist clenching or pounding	Aggression
Hand covering face	Protection, concealment
Covering eyes with hand	Fear or shame

Truthfulness

Truthfulness, also known as honesty and sincerity, is signaled by an acute memory, a perceptive recounting of facts, and a flowing narration. Truthful interviewees display a consistent recollection of details and attempt to dig up related specifics, often offering more information than they are asked for. With encouragement, they remember facts they thought they had forgotten. They will allow the interviewer to see their mental wheels moving in search of additional details. With the truthful, you might witness a furrowed brow, squinted eyes, and a contemplative silence. They are open and relaxed in their manner of speech, though they may be somewhat uneasy. In addition, they clearly explain the sequence of events, wanting to be correct.

The fundamentals of human personality are needs, emotions, thinking, and the ability to relate thoughts and feelings.[7] Our actions are a result and composite of all of these elements. But most of all, it is the satisfaction of essential and predictable needs that motivates every type of human behavior. Individuals try to satisfy their needs by maintaining physical comfort, avoiding the unsafe, attempting to gain understanding, detesting anonymity, desiring to be free from boredom, fearing the unknown, and hating disorder. Because social needs are comparatively unsatisfied, they have become a primary motivator for behavior. Interviewees desperately seek approval and reassurance that they are in control. Interviewees who feel threatened, inferior, or ridiculous will try to increase feelings of security, acceptance, and self-regard. Everyone experiences feelings of inferiority from time to time. You may succeed in gaining the cooperation of interviewees if you nourish them with feelings of security, friendship, and dignity and encourage them as they strive to satisfy their needs.

As we strive, directly or indirectly, to satisfy our needs, we have urges to behave in ways that will help or hinder our striving. Complications may develop as we seek to satisfy our needs. Either we modify our behavior to overcome the obstacles that are blocking the satisfaction of our needs, or we become frustrated at our failures. Frustration may provoke the emotional reactions of aggression, regression, and fixation as well as assorted defense mechanisms.

Refusal to Cooperate

At times, your efforts to gain the interviewee's cooperation will be unsuccessful. Interviewees might refuse to become involved in an investigation because they fear callous or indifferent treatment from legal authorities, fear of reprisal from the guilty party or others, inconvenience and financial loss, and confusion over legal proceedings. To some interviewees, court appearances entail an unnecessary burden on their time and energy. Whatever the interviewee's reason for not being cooperative, it is the skillful investigator that can build rapport with the person to get him to talk about things he was prepared not to discuss.

Physiological Signs

It is not unusual for the deceptive person to exhibit symptoms of physical shock while answering questions. These symptoms include lightheadedness and numbness in the extremities due to reduced blood circulation. These

[7] Maslow & Lowery, 1998, Changing Minds.org "The hierarchical effect". March 17, 2013.

physiological symptoms may be a response to the interviewee's feeling of being trapped and not knowing what to do. When they're lying, interviewees may also exhibit physiological cues such as burping, sweating, crying, and appearing to be in a state of turmoil. Truthful individuals generally do not undergo such stress when questioned, particularly when the interviewer remains calm and restrained.

Psychological Motives for Deception

Interviewees are deceptive for a variety of motives, frequently multiple motives. For some, the interview is an exercise in survival. The truth might result in consequences that would cause the interviewee shame, embarrassment, and punishment. How interviewees evaluate the hazards in any given interview is up to the individual being questioned and depends on what they have to hide. For other people, the interview is a game. The punishment and shame associated with getting caught are not as important as matching wits with the investigator. They make it their challenge to outsmart the interviewer. Much more could be said regarding the psychological motives behind deception, but in one form or another, these motives are woven among the interviewee's efforts to satisfy basic human needs.

The Pathological Liar

Pathological liars habitually tell lies so exaggerated or bizarre that they are suggestive of mental disorder. They fabricate when it would be simpler and more convenient to tell the truth. Their stories are often complex rationalizations leading to self-vindication. Most likely, pathological liars have been fabricating stories since childhood, so they might be so good at lying that they actually believe those lies. As interviewees, pathological liars are quite convincing when they say they did not just say what they actually did say. Most have the ability to refute your recall and notes pertaining to their comments. When faced with what they said only moments before, they will say something like, "Oh, no, I didn't say that!" This is when you have a reality check with yourself to see if you have lost your grip on the here and now. You know that you know what they said, but you check your notes to be sure. This is not the time to enter into an I-said-you-said game with the interviewee. Be strong and restrain your inclination to do battle, because you will lose in the end. After all, if you want information you can use, you can't win such a battle and expect friendly cooperation.

The Psychopathic Personality

The psychopathic personality develops along asocial and amoral lines and cannot adjust to society's standards. The psychopath is supremely selfish, living only for immediate gratification and without regard for the consequences. Normal individuals often sacrifice for the possibilities of the future and show a willingness to defer certain gratifications. The psychopath is always able to differentiate between right and wrong and usually is well acquainted with the requirements of society and religion, but he is absolutely unwilling to be governed by these laws. In fact, he may say that they do not concern him. The only interest he has in laws is to see that he is not caught when he violates them and, if he is caught, to try to secure, by some trick, a minimum punishment. Thus, one of the symptoms of being a psychopath is a complete selfishness that manifests itself in every act of the person. The only one the psychopath thinks of—in fact, the only individual that he completely loves—is himself, and he is surprisingly hardened to the rest of the world, including the members of his own family.

There is no satisfactory treatment for a psychopathic personality. Psychiatrists have so far been unable to do any good once the person's psychopathic behavior pattern has been established. Neither a long term in prison nor restraint in a psychiatric hospital can affect the conduct of psychopaths. Appearing self-assured, psychopaths are often cunning and convincing liars. Their motivation is to outsmart the investigator.

Rationalization

Interviewees, like all of us, act in accordance with their own individual, rational, reasoning powers. They protect themselves with rationalizations when they hold hidden images; thus they use rationalization to justify their behavior.

Everyone wants to feel capable, normal, and worthwhile compared to others. Few people are self-confident enough to be completely indifferent to insults and criticisms. People maintain their self-image by conforming to social pressure, which can produce feelings of conflict and guilt when group behavior contradicts the dictates of their own conscience. Hence interviewees will rationalize their actions, not wanting to expose themselves. By accepting their rationalizations, you can help interviewees feel more confident and lessen their feelings of self-doubt. As a result, you might be more likely to gain their cooperation.

You can encourage interviewees to cooperate through active listening, building rapport, asking the right questions, and being prepared. Try to eliminate negative aspects of the situation that might show signs of disgust or disappointment, to reduce the interviewee's reluctance to cooperate. You might suggest that the interviewee's action (or lack of action) is not so unique after all and that many people would take the same action if they found themselves in those circumstances. Although you are diminishing the significance of her acts, you are not changing the interviewee's overall responsibility for her actions nor overlooking the effect her actions had on others. Your goal is always to allow for the free flow of accurate information.

You might need to help some interviewees rationalize their cooperation with the investigation. Cooperation may cause them to lose face if it cannot be justified. If low self-esteem is the price of assisting with an investigation, some interviewees will refuse.

Projection

Humans try to appear reasonable to themselves and to others by doing what is proper and acceptable. Some people use the defense mechanism of projection to shift onto others the responsibilities that they themselves have not adequately handled. When they cannot live up to expectations, they blame other people or the situation itself for their behavior. They use projection to make their behavior understandable and socially acceptable. Thus, it is always someone else's fault. Often interviewees project their blame onto others in their effort to save face.

Skilled interviewers use deductive logic when reaching a conclusion about the interviewee's truthfulness. When interviewing, you will need to consider the subject's verbal and nonverbal behavior equally. The interviewer's tactics are based on generalizations accumulated from personal experience.

Concluding That There Has Been Deception

Concluding that your interviewee was truthful or deceptive will be based on all parts of the interview, verbal and nonverbal, and the personal experience of the interviewer. The interviewer will weigh the totality of the interview and look for a baseline to help indicate truthfulness or deception.

REVIEW QUESTIONS

1. Does the concept of deception have the same meaning to everyone throughout the world?
2. Define the terms *esteem* and *self-esteem*.

3. How do interviewees try to protect their self-image?
4. What is the relationship between needs and human behavior?
5. What can you do to influence the interviewee's behavior?
6. Why would a person resist answering your questions about someone else?
7. How does an understanding of the interviewee's needs help you achieve your objective?
8. What is the best response to an interviewee's anger?
9. What are the four tests of interviewee credibility?
10. How do the truthful typically answer questions?
11. What is deception?
12. Why are convincing liars difficult to detect?
13. Identify several verbal, nonverbal, and physiological signs of deception.
14. What is the significance of an interviewee's responding with objections rather than denials?
15. How does a deceptive person's eye contact differ from that of the truthful person?
16. List three key characteristics of a psychopath.
17. Contrast rationalization and projection.
18. Why do people rationalize?
19. Why do pathological liars lie? Why do other people lie?
20. On what should you base your conclusion as to an interviewee's truthfulness?

CHAPTER 5

Evidence

Competent evidence is evidence that has been properly collected, identified, filed, and continuously secured.

All clues and all traces of evidence are valuable in solving a crime. Even small bits of evidence may help prove someone's guilt, whereas limiting the search for evidence may lead to charging the wrong person with the crime. Therefore, the search for guilt or innocence arises out of the examination of all available evidence.

REAL, DOCUMENTARY, AND TESTIMONIAL EVIDENCE

There are three basic types of evidence. *Real* and *documentary* evidence make up about 20 percent of all evidence presented in courts of law; *testimonial* evidence accounts for the remaining 80 percent.

Real, or *physical*, *evidence* is something you can photograph, chart, put your hands on, pick up, or store. It consists of tangible items such as a bullet, a tire track, a key, a cell phone, or a fingerprint. Real evidence is usually found at a crime scene and pertains to the way the crime was committed and who is culpable. It is not based on the memory of the interviewee, unless the evidence was found because a witness recalled where the shooter threw the gun or where the robber touched the bank counter. Such evidence is often volatile, fragile, and fleeting. It requires expert handling if it is to be useful in court.

In handling real evidence, the investigator must maintain a *chain of custody*, which records how the evidence was handled, to prove that it was not contaminated in any way. *Documentary evidence*, on the other hand, is usually not found at a crime scene. Especially with crimes of passion, such as murder and assault, documentary evidence is collected after the crime scene investigation has been completed. Documentary evidence often consists of a record or an account that will help investigators prove or disprove some fact. It includes such things as credit card receipts, hotel registers, and business records or computers. Like real evidence, documentary evidence has substance. One difference is that real evidence is created as a byproduct of a crime, whereas documentary evidence is often mandated or regulated in some way, such as records maintained in the normal course of business.

In many criminal investigations such as cases of fraud or embezzlement, documents are the main form of evidence. Investigators of such white-collar crimes make a special effort to legally and quickly collect documents to preserve them as evidence. Often search warrants or subpoenas are required to obtain stored business documents.

The part played by documentary evidence in an investigation is based on what the document contains. For example, data entered into a diary by a victim, a witness, or a suspect or a text message received on an iPhone could be vital corroboration of other evidence discovered in other ways through such data contained in telephone records, receipts, and so forth. Motel records might verify that a person was a guest at a particular motel on a particular day, as stated on credit card records. Other documents might confirm that a person was at a certain place at a particular time or was engaged in a specified activity.

Testimonial evidence generally comes from interviews of victims, witnesses, and suspects. It is given verbally but might subsequently be recorded in written form. Admissions and confessions gained through the interrogation of a subject are one kind of testimonial evidence.

Interviewing is the primary method of collecting testimonial evidence. Interviews are different from interrogations in that their objectives differ. The goal of interviewing is to collect truthful data to be used for informed decision making and for taking action. An interrogation, on the other hand, is a face-to-face meeting with a subject with the distinct objective of gaining an admission or a confession related to a real or apparent violation of law or policy.

VOLUNTARY CONFESSIONS

If you are a private investigator, a corporate investigator, or a security manager, you will want to get a written confession after a suspect makes a verbal confession. This written confession will be a statement detailing all the facts of the case that the interviewee can recall. If you work for a law enforcement agency or a federal agency, you are required to give a suspect a *Miranda warning*.[1] The confession must still be voluntary but obtained after the suspect was given a *Miranda* warning or the confession will be rejected as evidence at a trial or administrative hearing. Before a person in police custody or otherwise deprived of freedom "in any significant way" may be interviewed or interrogated, *Miranda* warnings must be given (*Miranda v. Arizona*

---

[1] http://usgovinfo.about.com/cs/mirandarights/a/miranda_2.htm.

[1966]). The exact wording of the *Miranda* rights statement is not specified in the Supreme Court's historic decision. Instead, law enforcement agencies have created a basic set of simple statements that can be read to accused persons prior to any questioning. Here are paraphrased examples of the basic *Miranda* rights statements, along with related excerpts from the Supreme Court decision:

1. You have the right to remain silent.
2. Anything you say can be used against you in a court of law.
3. You have the right to have an attorney present now and during any future questioning.
4. If you cannot afford an attorney, one will be appointed to you free of charge if you wish.
5. Do you understand these rights?

These warnings have come to be known as the *Miranda warnings*, after the U.S. Supreme Court case in which they were enumerated. The *Miranda* warnings apply *only* to "investigative custodial questioning aimed at eliciting evidence of a crime." Subjects in custody must understand what they are being told. The investigator is not permitted to bully a suspect into talking once they decide not to do so, nor may the investigator attempt to dissuade a suspect from speaking with a lawyer. This ensures that subjects in custody know that they have the right to remain silent.[2] After receiving the required warnings and expressing willingness to answer questions, a subject in custody may legally be interrogated. It is unnecessary to embellish the *Miranda* warnings or to add new warnings. Similarly, it is unnecessary to use the exact language contained in *Miranda*.

In Canada, equivalent rights exist pursuant to the Charter of Rights and Freedoms. If arrested, a person has the right to:

1. Be informed promptly of the reasons therefor
2. Retain and instruct counsel without delay and be informed of that right
3. Have the validity of the detention determined by way of *habeas corpus* and to be released if the detention is not lawful

Around the world, other countries have a standard letter of rights, similar to the U.S. *Miranda* warning that is given to criminal suspects in police custody before an interrogation begins.

To ensure that a confession holds up in court, follow proper procedures for interviewing the subject. If you are in the public sector, you must make it clear when a suspect is not under arrest and must document that the suspect is

---

[2] *Harryman v. Estelle*, 1980.

free to leave if he or she so desires. If the inquiry is held in an official location, such as a police station, it is imperative that interviewees comprehend that they are not being detained or in custody, if such is the case. Voluntary response is vital in these matters. To fight the admissibility of a confession in court, defense attorneys sometimes argue that psychological coercion was used to obtain the confession.

Some investigators earnestly urge the subject to grant permission for the interrogation; other investigators, directly or indirectly, strongly advise the subject not to grant permission. As you give the warnings, use a neutral tone and a matter-of-fact manner. This is not a time to caution, suggest, frighten, or admonish the person in custody.

Let's take a minute to examine the words *interview* and *interrogation,* because they will undoubtedly come up throughout this book and throughout your career as an investigative interviewer. An *interview* is a nonaccusatory question-and-answer session with anyone you are trying to obtain information from— witnesses, suspects, or victims. If you recall, the successful interview is one that collects accurate and useful information. Some of the questions may be of an investigative nature, some to elicit behavioral responses. The interviewer is building rapport and maintaining a nonaccusatory tone and demeanor throughout the interview. The skilled interviewer will ask questions that produce a narrative answer rather than a yes-or-no response. Because of the nature of the questions, the interviewee will do most of the talking. The only information gathered should come from the interviewee.

An *interrogation* is often used to elicit the truth from a person the investigator believes has lied during an interview. There may come a point in the interview that it turns from an interview into an interrogation or the other way around. It will depend on the interviewee as to the information he gives up or the information he is hiding. An interviewer that is skilled will be able to take it from an interview to an interrogation and then back when necessary. It takes practice to be able to read a person and then determine your strategy. We will talk more about practice, preparation, and skill throughout the book.

When the *Miranda* Warnings Are Required

In 1976, the Supreme Court removed the misconception that *Miranda* warnings must be given to anyone upon whom suspicion is "focused."[3] Rather, the Court said, the warnings are required only when the subject is in police custody.

[3] *Beckwith v. United States*, 1976; Inbau et al., 1986

In an earlier case, the Court had defined "in police custody or otherwise deprived of freedom in any significant way" (the wording used in *Miranda v. Arizona* [1966]). The Court said that the key elements are "the time of the interrogation, the number of officers involved, and the apparent formal arrest of the subject" (*Orozco v. Texas* [1969]).

Regarding noncustodial interviewing within a police facility, the Supreme Court held that a noncustodial situation does not require the *Miranda* warnings simply because a reviewing court concludes that, even in the absence of any formal arrest or restraint of freedom of movement, the questioning took place in a "coercive environment" (*Oregon v. Mathiason* [1977]). The Court considered the circumstances of the interrogation when it provided this opinion:

> Any interview of one suspected of a crime by a police officer will have coercive aspects to it, simply by virtue of the fact that the police officer is part of a law enforcement system which may ultimately cause the suspect to be charged with a crime. But police officers are not required to administer Miranda warnings to everyone whom they question. Nor is the requirement of warnings to be imposed simply because the questioning takes place in the station house, or because the questioned person is one whom the police suspect. Miranda warnings are required only where there has been such a restriction on a person's freedom as to render him "in custody." It was that sort of coercive environment to which Miranda by its terms was made applicable and to which it is limited.

Legally, *interrogation* is defined as asking a question, making a comment, displaying an object, or presenting a police report if this action calls for a response that may be incriminating. The subtle use of these actions makes them "functional equivalents" of direct questions asked during an interrogation (*Brewer v. Williams* [1977]). This means that they, too, are bound by *Miranda*, but an exception can be found in *Rhode Island v. Innes* (1980).

If suspects who are not in custody freely consent to be interviewed or interrogated, there is no requirement that they be given the *Miranda* warnings. If an interviewee begins to confess without being interrogated, let him or her continue without interruption. When the confession has concluded, give the *Miranda* warnings to prevent any court from holding that custody began at the conclusion of the confession.

Subjects in custody can waive their constitutional rights. This is usually done in writing and is signed, but oral waivers will suffice.

Police officers working private or part-time positions are bound by the *Miranda* ruling. If you are not conducting the investigation as a police officer, the *Miranda* decision does not affect you unless you are acting in cooperation with the police as a police agent. It's important to realize, however, that regardless of your role as an investigator, if you compel someone to confess, you are coercing a confession that will not hold up as legal evidence. Private security investigators generally do not have to administer *Miranda* warnings.

LEGAL TACTICS USED IN SEEKING A CONFESSION

Be fair and practical in interrogating or interviewing anyone, particularly suspects in custody. It is vital to avoid saying or doing anything that might cause an innocent person to confess. Do not use coercion, intimidation, threats, promises, or duress to force a confession; such action is neither legal nor acceptable. Intimidation reaps resentment, not truthful cooperation. Different parts of the world have different ethical standards and techniques; not all techniques used in some countries would be considered fair and professional in North America. Such tactics are self-defeating and inappropriate.

The following legal tactics can be used during an interrogation:
- Exhibit confidence in the subject's culpability.
- Present circumstantial evidence to persuade the subject to tell the truth.
- Observe the subject's behavior for indications of deception.
- Empathize with and help the subject rationalize his or her actions and save face.
- Minimize the significance of the matter under investigation.
- Offer nonjudgmental acceptance of the subject's behavior.
- Point out the futility of not telling the truth.
- Follow your senses and intuition.

Trickery and deceit are often used in interrogations. The U.S. Supreme Court gave recognition to the necessity of these tactics in Frazier v Cupp (1969). The Court held: "The fact that the police misrepresented the statements that [a suspected accomplice] had made is, while relevant, insufficient in our view to make this otherwise voluntary confession inadmissible. These cases must be decided by viewing the 'totality of the circumstances.'"

EVIDENCE COLLECTION AND PRESERVATION

Strict rules govern the handling of all evidence before it is presented in court. The court that ultimately hears the evidence will want to know whether it was obtained legally, who handled it before it reached the court, and how it was handled. Does the evidence bear directly on the case, and does it accurately represent what happened? Was it tampered with in any way? Is it tainted? Before you begin to hunt for evidence, you must know what you're searching for, and that, in turn, depends on the objective of your investigation. If your objective is to prove intent in some criminal, civil, or administrative investigation, you may be looking for documents bearing a certain date or signature. If it is a hit-and-run case, the evidence may be skid marks or broken car parts on the road. When interviewing an eyewitness, you may be searching for what the person heard or saw at the crime scene.

There is a difference, of course, between knowing what type of evidence you are looking for and searching only for evidence that suits some preconceived notion of who is culpable. Although having a theory or being guided by probabilities is generally acceptable, twisting the evidence to distort the truth is not. Professional investigators strive to maintain a neutral manner and an open mind so that they can impartially collect all available evidence.

If you obtain an admission or a confession, you will be challenged about how you obtained it. Did you determine that the interviewee was lying based on your intuition and observations? As you collect evidence, be sure to make every effort to ensure that all evidence is obtained legally. In deciding whether to admit testimonial evidence, courts consider who was present, what was said, and how it was said. If evidence is contaminated by coercive tactics, threats, or illegal promises, we can expect a court to throw it out.

Even though you may collect massive amounts of evidence, not all of it will be pertinent to your investigation. You could interview 50 people and find only two who have useful information. Details of the other 48 interviews should not play a significant role in your report other than a notation that the interviews took place.

All evidence—real, documentary, and testimonial—can become contaminated. Preserving evidence and protecting it from contamination are vital to its successful presentation in court.

The following is a list of the types of evidence you should look for:
- Ammunition
- Arson, accelerants used
- Assault, blood, DNA analysis, and DNA profiling
- Blood splatters
- Barcodes
- Bite marks
- Body fluids
- Burglary, tools, and tool marks
- Computer
- *Corpus delicti*

- Cell phone and text messages
- Social networks
- Drugs
- Fibers and laundry marks or dry cleaning marks
- Fingerprints
- Glasses
- Hair
- Rope and rope knots
- Wood, paint, and cement
- Sex cases, rape kit exam
- Shoe impressions
- Tire or wheel impressions
- Material sent to the FBI lab
- Answering machine and voice prints
- Soil
- Weapons
- Forensic science characteristics
- Graffiti
- Computers, iPhones, iPads, Kindles
- Keys

The investigation and gathering of evidence *are both a science as well as an art*. Investigators and interviewers today need to have more skills than merely a badge and a gun. You have to have a head for facts, you have to have to think outside the box and you need to have persistence, dedication, instinct, and patience.

REPORT WRITING

Often, reports are official documents that detail how evidence was collected and preserved during an investigation. Hence they are an important part of the chain of custody.

The technique of report writing can be learned by anyone who possesses two basic qualities: fundamental communication skills and a trained ability to observe. To be a competent investigator, you must write reports clearly so that everyone who reads them will know what you did and why. Often the report is needed long after the crime and must be interpreted by many people unfamiliar with the crime. Interviewers must write the report so that the prosecutor and courts can fully understand what took place.

Clear expression is not difficult to achieve, but it does take practice. Always write just the facts when you are taking notes or writing your report.

A statement is the literal reproduction of the actual words spoken by the interviewee. Be a creative listener, use skillful phrases, and ask questions politely. First listen, and then write notes. Be supportive and encouraging.

There are five basic steps in writing a report as listed below.

1. Gather the facts (investigate, interview, interrogate). What are you going to tell us?
2. Take notes and record the facts as soon as possible
3. Organize the facts; create an outline and bullet points.
4. Write the report—just the facts. Decide how many words you want to write for each part of the report.
5. Edit and revise your report.

Good notes are a prerequisite for a good report, and they share many of the characteristics of a good report. When you're taking notes, organize your information, then report it in chronologically arranged paragraphs. Keep your writing straightforward and simple.

Characteristics of a Well-Written Report

A well-written report indicates that you have done your job and that you recognize your responsibilities to your client, corporation, or community. A well-written report reflects positively on your education, your competence, and your professionalism, and it communicates better than a poorly prepared report.

Well-written reports share the following characteristics:

*   *Factual.* Facts make up the backbone of all reports. A fact is a statement that can be verified and known as a certainty. *Black's Law Dictionary* defines a fact as a thing done; an action performed or an incident transpiring; an event or circumstance; an actual occurrence. Present your facts, draw your conclusion, and stipulate which is which. A well-written report does not contain unidentified opinions.
*   *Accurate.* Just as there are rules for spelling, capitalization, and punctuation, there are rules for word choice. Ensure accuracy by being specific in your language and by choosing the most appropriate words for each situation. Avoid jargon, which creates confusion.
*   *Objective.* A good report is fair and impartial. Subjective writing might be more colorful than objective writing, but it has no place in a report. You can ensure objectivity in your reports by including all relevant facts and by avoiding words with emotional overtones. Specific types of crime require different information, but you will frequently need certain

general information. You will want to include the *who, what, when,* and *where* questions that should be answered by factual statements. The *how* and *why* statements may require inferences on your part. When this is the case, and especially when addressing the question of motive, clearly label your opinions. Avoid personal opinions.

- *Complete.* A report should give as full an account as possible. To avoid slanting your report, record all possible motives reported to you, no matter how implausible they may seem.
- *Concise.* The information you choose to include should be worded as concisely as possible; no one wants to read a wordy report. You can reduce wordiness two ways: (1) Leave out unnecessary information, and (2) use as few words as possible to record the necessary facts. Avoid vague phrases such as "a long time ago" or "sometime in the winter." You need to create a detailed report, and these phrases do not provide such detail.
- *Clear.* Clarity, one of the most important characteristics of a well-written report.
- *Mechanically correct.* Be sure to use correct spelling, capitalization, and punctuation in your report. A report riddled with errors in these areas gives a poor impression of its writer and the writer's actions.
- *Written in standard English.* When you translate your ideas into words, follow the rules for correct writing. Use the past tense, complete sentences, and good grammar. Keep your sentences short and language simple and concise. Do not use jargon or texting phrases that are not complete sentences.
- *Legible.* An illegible report gives a poor impression of the writer and a distorted explanation of who said what. Reread and edit your report, or even better, have another person proofread your report for accuracy and grammatical errors.
- *On time.* A report that is submitted late reflects negatively on the report writer.

Make your reports, like all your other communications, as clear and direct as possible. The following suggestions will help ensure that your reports can be easily understood:

- Use the first person. That is, write *I* instead of *the investigator* or *the interviewer.* First-person writing is recommended for law enforcement reports because it is direct.
- Write in past tense throughout your report.
- Write in active voice. For example, say, "I asked Jane Smith . . ." rather than "Jane Smith was asked . . .." The active voice clearly indicates who performed the action.

- Be objective.
- Correctly modify details to be included.
- When using pronouns, be sure it is clear to whom they refer.
- Don't use police lingo.
- Don't use slang.
- Use parallelism. That is, use the same type of structure for similar parts of a sentence.
- Choose your words carefully. Avoid legal, technical, unfamiliar, and slang words.
- Include specific, concrete facts and details.
- Keep descriptive words and phrases as close as possible to the words they describe. Use correct grammar.
- Use diagrams and sketches to clarify a complex description.
- Quality reports are always typed, using paragraphs, past tense, and first person. Remember that all reports are a permanent written record of your case.

TESTIMONY IN A COURT OF LAW

Testimonial evidence is the foundation of both criminal and civil litigation and is often the subject of cross-examination. Evidence presented for consideration in court cannot intentionally be tainted. It cannot be tampered with and still be credible and trustworthy. True professionals maintain the integrity of the evidence and deserve society's honor and respect.

During a trial, attorneys often seek to impeach, or discredit, witnesses for the opposing side. Most states allow the credibility of a witness to be attacked during a trial. This is usually done by challenging the truthfulness and consistency of the witness's statements. Investigators are obligated to tell the truth, whether in court or when giving a legal deposition. "From the opposing attorney's point of view, the purpose of the deposition is to create a record for future impeachment." The deposition process can be a lengthy one. Be patient. Hide your desire to get it over with. You will need to show toughness, resolve, and a willingness to stay as long as necessary.[4]

---

[4] Jack v. Matson, pp. 41–42.

REVIEW QUESTIONS

1. Identify the three types of evidence and give two examples of each.
2. What is the difference between interviewing and interrogating?
3. Why must a confession be voluntary, and what might happen if a confession is not obtained voluntarily?
4. What are the four *Miranda* warnings?
5. When are we legally required to give the *Miranda* warnings? Discuss specific situations.
6. How has the U.S. Supreme Court defined interrogation?
7. Is a confession legal if a private security person compels someone to confess?
8. Identify at least three legal interrogation tactics.
9. Is it permissible to use trickery when trying to obtain a confession?
10. Why is it important for the court to consider "the totality of the circumstances" under which evidence is located, collected, and preserved?
11. List the five basic steps in writing a report.
12. What are the 10 characteristics of a well-written report?
13. What is a fact?
14. How can you ensure objectivity in your reports?
15. What can you do to make your reports clear?

CHAPTER 6

Public and Private Interviewing

Whether from the public or private sector, first-class investigators resemble each other more than they differ. They are successful because they share well-practiced skills, a high degree of perception, and a positive attitude. For the purposes of this chapter, we define *public* investigators as official law enforcement agents, such as state or local police officers. We define *private* investigators as licensed private detectives, private investigators, asset protection, security management, or loss prevention specialists. Although the number of investigators in the public sector generally remains steady, the number of investigators in the private sector is growing. This chapter reviews some distinctions between the kinds of crimes public and private detectives investigate (with particular attention to white-collar crime) and the procedures they follow.

The fundamental difference between public and private investigations is the *objective*. In the public sector, the objective is to serve the interests of society.[1] The primary objective of the investigative process in the private sector is to serve the interests of the organization, company, or client that employs the investigator. What might serve the best interests of society may differ from what might be in the best interests of the organization or client. In the private sector, my primary concern as a private investigator might be recovering an asset or obtaining a statement. Since I would be working for a client, my tasks or project will be defined by the client. In the public sector, the main concern is prosecution. In the public sector, the investigator knows that the victim is society, whereas the private investigator's victim could be the shareholders of a company or an organization.

Various perceptions and objectives have a direct impact on the strategies and character of the investigation process. This leads to other differences in the interviewing process as well, such as choices and decisions based on whether this is a private investigation or a public one. The public investigator represents the sovereignty of government, the authority of which is vested in laws, both constitutional and statutory. The source of funding is ultimately through taxation, whereas the private investigator is hired by management. Although state, federal, and corporate laws must be followed,

---

[1] Louis A. Tyska, CPP, and Lawrence J. Fennelly, *Investigations: 150 Things You Should Know*, 1999.

there are plenty of differences, including limitations on government records, authority, detention, interview process, Miranda warning, and arrest.

REPORTING AND CLASSIFYING CRIME

Before we continue, let's take a brief look at how crime is reported and classified. We will look at the United States, Canada, and the United Nations-affiliated European Institute for Crime Prevention and Control.

The Criminal Code of Canada sets out three main offense classifications, which are as follows:

1. Purely summary conviction offenses. These offenses are the most minor.
2. Purely indictable offense, the most serious offenses. The majority of criminal charges in Canada are hybrid offenses such as DUI and assault charges.
3. Hybrid offenses, more serious than the most minor, follow the summary conviction offenses. These proceed summarily (less serious) or by indictment (more serious), depending on the classification the prosecutor chooses.

Canada has a Uniform Crime Reporting Survey (UCR) that was designed to measure the incidence of crime in Canada and its characteristics. This survey is used by federal and provincial policy makers. The Canadian Centre for Justice Statistics (CCJS) collects police-reported crime statistics through the Uniform Crime Reporting Survey.

In Europe there are several agencies that collect crime data:

- European Institute for Crime Prevention and Control, Affiliated with the United Nations (HEUNI), located in Finland.
- The United Nations Office on Drugs and Crime (UNODC), located in Vienna, Austria, collects data on crime and provides analysis to the international community. The UNODC works on developing standards for national crime and criminal justice information systems and for victimization surveys. Through collecting periodic reports on selected crime issues, they can provide in-depth analysis on issues that are global and regional. Another initiative is Data for Africa, which collects and analyzes data and trends in drugs, crime, and victimization in African countries.
- The United Nations Survey on Crime Trends and Operations Criminal Justice Systems (abbreviated as UN-CTS) collect basic information on recorded crime and on resources of criminal justice systems in member regions such as Europe and North America.

In the United States, city, county, and state law enforcement agencies keep track of the yearly incidence of various crimes in their jurisdictions. Compiled by volume and frequency, these statistics are sent to the Federal Bureau of Investigation (FBI), which issues the annual *Uniform Crime Report*. The FBI classifies the most serious crimes, such as murder, rape, and robbery, as *Part I offenses*. These crimes, which are the most likely to be reported to the police, serve as the major index of crime in the United States. The crimes listed as *Part II offenses* are considered less serious—that is, less harmful to individuals and less damaging to society. The FBI considers fraud and embezzlement to be Part II offenses. The federal guidelines define fraud as "fraudulent conversion and obtaining money or property by false pretenses (confidence games and bad checks, except forgeries and counterfeiting, are included)" and embezzlement as "the misappropriation or misapplication of money or property entrusted to one's care, custody, or control." Fraud and embezzlement cost U.S. businesses billions of dollars each year. To control their losses, many companies have established their own security or loss prevention staffs to investigate these crimes. More often than not, the police are never notified when these crimes occur.

Offense Definitions

This section is reprinted, with permission, from Appendix II - Offenses in Uniform Crime Reporting, from Crime in the US 2004, Department of Justice, FBI. The Uniform Crime Reporting (UCR) Program divides offenses into two groups: Part I and Part II crimes. Each month, participating law enforcement agencies submit information on the number of Part I offenses that become known to them; those offenses cleared by arrest or exceptional means; and the age, sex, and race of persons arrested for each of the offenses. Contributors provide only arrest data for Part II offenses.

The UCR Program collects data about Part I offenses to measure the level and scope of crime occurring throughout the nation. The program's founders chose these offenses because they are serious crimes, they occur with regularity in all areas of the country, and they are likely to be reported to police. The Part I offenses are as follows:

- *Criminal homicide.* (a) Murder and nonnegligent manslaughter: the willful (nonnegligent) killing of one human being by another. Deaths caused by negligence, attempts to kill, assaults to kill, suicides, and accidental deaths are excluded. The program classifies justifiable homicides separately and limits the definition to: (1) the killing of a felon by a law enforcement officer in the line of duty; or (2) the killing of a felon, during the commission of a felony, by a private citizen. (b) Manslaughter by negligence:

The killing of another person through gross negligence. Deaths of persons due to their own negligence, accidental deaths not resulting from gross negligence, and traffic fatalities are not included in the category of manslaughter by negligence.

- *Forcible rape.* The carnal knowledge of a female, forcibly and against her will. Rapes by force and attempts or assaults to rape, regardless of the age of the victim, are included. Statutory offenses (no force used—victim under age of consent) are excluded.
- *Robbery.* The taking or attempting to take anything of value from the care, custody, or control of a person or persons by force or threat of force or violence and/or by putting the victim in fear.
- *Aggravated assault.* An unlawful attack by one person upon another for the purpose of inflicting severe or aggravated bodily injury. This type of assault usually is accompanied by the use of a weapon or by means likely to produce death or great bodily harm. Simple assaults are excluded.
- *Burglary (breaking or entering).* The unlawful entry of a structure to commit a felony or a theft. Attempted forcible entry is included.
- *Larceny; theft (except motor vehicle theft).* The unlawful taking, carrying, leading, or riding away of property from the possession or constructive possession of another. Examples are thefts of bicycles, motor vehicle parts and accessories, shoplifting, pocket picking, or the stealing of any property or article that is not taken by force and violence or by fraud. Attempted larcenies are included. Embezzlement, confidence games, forgery, check fraud, etc. are excluded.
- *Motor vehicle theft.* The theft or attempted theft of a motor vehicle. A motor vehicle is self-propelled and runs on land surface and not on rails. Motorboats, construction equipment, airplanes, and farming equipment are specifically excluded from this category.
- *Arson.* Any willful or malicious burning or attempt to burn, with or without intent to defraud, a dwelling house, public building, motor vehicle or aircraft, personal property of another, etc.

The Part II offenses, for which only arrest data are collected, are:

- *Other assaults (simple).* Assaults and attempted assaults where no weapon was used or no serious or aggravated injury resulted to the victim. Stalking, intimidation, coercion, and hazing are included.
- *Forgery and counterfeiting.* The altering, copying, or imitating of something, without authority or right, with the intent to deceive or defraud by passing the copy or thing altered or imitated as that which is original or genuine; or the selling, buying, or possession of an altered, copied, or

imitated thing with the intent to deceive or defraud. Attempts are included.

- *Fraud.* The intentional perversion of the truth for the purpose of inducing another person or other entity in reliance upon it to part with something of value or to surrender a legal right. Fraudulent conversion and obtaining of money or property by false pretenses. Confidence games and bad checks, except forgeries and counterfeiting, are included.
- *Embezzlement.* The unlawful misappropriation or misapplication by an offender to his/her own use or purpose of money, property, or some other thing of value entrusted to his/her care, custody, or control.
- *Stolen property—buying, receiving, possessing.* Buying, receiving, possessing, selling, concealing, or transporting any property with the knowledge that it has been unlawfully taken, as by burglary, embezzlement, fraud, larceny, robbery, etc. Attempts are included.
- *Vandalism.* To willfully or maliciously destroy, injure, disfigure, or deface any public or private property, real or personal, without the consent of the owner or person having custody or control by cutting, tearing, breaking, marking, painting, drawing, covering with filth, or any other such means as may be specified by local law. Attempts are included.
- *Weapons—carrying, possessing, etc.* The violation of laws or ordinances prohibiting the manufacture, sale, purchase, transportation, possession, concealment, or use of firearms, cutting instruments, explosives, incendiary devices, or other deadly weapons. Attempts are included.
- *Prostitution and commercialized vice.* The unlawful promotion of or participation in sexual activities for profit, including attempts. To solicit customers or transport persons for prostitution purposes; to own, manage, or operate a dwelling or other establishment for the purpose of providing a place where prostitution is performed; or to otherwise assist or promote prostitution.
- *Sex offenses (except forcible rape, prostitution, and commercialized vice).* Offenses against chastity, common decency, morals, and the like. Incest, indecent exposure, and statutory rape are included. Attempts are included.
- *Drug abuse violations.* The violation of laws prohibiting the production, distribution, and/or use of certain controlled substances. The unlawful cultivation, manufacture, distribution, sale, purchase, use, possession, transportation, or importation of any controlled drug or narcotic substance. Arrests for violations of state and local laws, specifically those relating to the unlawful possession, sale, use, growing, manufacturing, and making of narcotic drugs. The following drug categories are

specified: opium or cocaine and their derivatives (morphine, heroin, codeine); marijuana; synthetic narcotics—manufactured narcotics that can cause true addiction (demerol, methadone); and dangerous nonnarcotic drugs (barbiturates, benzedrine).

- *Gambling.* To unlawfully bet or wager money or something else of value; assist, promote, or operate a game of chance for money or some other stake; possess or transmit wagering information; manufacture, sell, purchase, possess, or transport gambling equipment, devices, or goods; or tamper with the outcome of a sporting event or contest to gain a gambling advantage.

- *Offenses against the family and children.* Unlawful nonviolent acts by a family member (or legal guardian) that threaten the physical, mental, or economic well-being or morals of another family member and that are not classifiable as other offenses, such as assault or sex offenses. Attempts are included.

- *Driving under the influence.* Driving or operating a motor vehicle or common carrier while mentally or physically impaired as the result of consuming an alcoholic beverage or using a drug or narcotic.

- *Liquor laws.* The violation of state or local laws or ordinances prohibiting the manufacture, sale, purchase, transportation, possession, or use of alcoholic beverages, not including driving under the influence and drunkenness. Federal violations are excluded.

- *Drunkenness.* To drink alcoholic beverages to the extent that one's mental faculties and physical coordination are substantially impaired. Driving under the influence is excluded.

- *Disorderly conduct.* Any behavior that tends to disturb the public peace or decorum, scandalize the community, or shock the public sense of morality.

- *Vagrancy.* The violation of a court order, regulation, ordinance, or law requiring the withdrawal of persons from the streets or other specified areas; prohibiting persons from remaining in an area or place in an idle or aimless manner; or prohibiting persons from going from place to place without visible means of support.

- *All other offenses.* All violations of state or local laws not specifically identified as Part I or Part II offenses, except traffic violations.

- *Suspicion.* Arrested for no specific offense and released without formal charges being placed.

- *Curfew and loitering laws (persons under age 18).* Violations by juveniles of local curfew or loitering ordinances.

According to the 2011 *Crime in the United States* report, the estimated number of violent crimes reported to law enforcement (1,203,564) decreased for the fifth year in a row, whereas the estimated number of property crimes reported to law enforcement (9,063,173) decreased for the ninth year in a row.[2]

VIOLENT CRIME

The South, the most populous region in the country, accounted for 41.3 percent of all violent crimes (lesser volumes of 22.9 percent were tallied in the West, 19.5 percent in the Midwest, and 16.2 percent in the Northeast).

- Aggravated assaults accounted for the highest number of estimated violent crimes reported to law enforcement at 62.4 percent.
- Firearms were used in 67.8 percent of the nation's murders, 41.3 percent of robberies, and 21.2 percent of aggravated assaults. (Data on weapons used during forcible rapes is not collected.)
- In 2011, 64.8 percent of murder offenses, 41.2 percent of forcible rape offenses, 28.7 percent of robbery offenses, and 56.9 percent of aggravated assault offenses were "cleared"—either by the arrest of the subject or because law enforcement encountered a circumstance beyond its control that prohibited an arrest after the subject was identified (i.e., death of the subject).

PROPERTY CRIME

Property crime which are crimes against property, in the US, are typically referred to criminal offenses such as burglary, larceny, fraud, embezzlement, forgery, car theft and arson. Another property crime offense, shoplifting, is a form of larceny. The property crime offense list is vast and can also be described as crimes against property/material based items.

- Data shows that 43.2 percent of the estimated property crimes occurred in the South (followed by the West with 22.8 percent, the Midwest with 21.1 percent, and the Northeast with 13.0 percent).
- Larceny-theft accounted for 68 percent of all property crimes in 2011.
- Property crimes resulted in estimated losses of $156.6 billion.
- Also cleared were 21.5 percent of larceny-theft offenses, 12.7 percent of burglary offenses, 11.9 percent of motor vehicle theft offenses, and 18.8 percent of arson offenses.

The FBI's Uniform Crime Reporting (UCR) program is one of two statistical programs administered by the Department of Justice that measure

[2] FBI website, www.fbi.gov, March 1, 2013.

the magnitude, nature, and impact of crime. The other is the National Crime Victimization Survey (NCVS), conducted by the Bureau of Justice Statistics.

The programs were designed to complement each other, providing valuable information about aspects of the nation's crime problem, but due to methodology and crime coverage differences, users should not compare crime trends between the two programs. The UCR program provides a reliable set of criminal justice statistics for law enforcement administration, operation, and management as well as to indicate fluctuations in the level of crime. The NCVS provides previously unavailable information about victims, offenders, and crime, including crimes not reported to police. Additional information about the differences between the two programs can be found in the "Nation's Two Crime Measures" section of *Crime in the United States*.

Looking ahead to 2013 and beyond, the UCR program is working to complete the automation of its data collection system, which will result in improved data collection efforts with new offense categories and revised offense definitions as well as a faster turnaround time to analyze and publish the data. In addition, beginning with the 2013 data, the new definition of rape will take effect; the FBI is developing options for law enforcement agencies to meet this requirement, which will be built into the new data collection system.

UCR's *Law Enforcement Officers Killed and Assaulted, 2011* and *Hate Crimes Statistics, 2011*

INVESTIGATIONS IN THE PUBLIC AND PRIVATE SPHERES

Traditionally, private investigators have dealt with fraud and embezzlement, whereas the police have handled the violent crimes of murder, rape, and assault. Until just recently, law enforcement officers were not properly trained to investigate sophisticated white-collar crimes. Rather, police training was reactive in nature, emphasizing how to diffuse violent situations, how to perform first aid, how to shoot straight, and such topics. The subtle aspects of human interaction, the gentle art of communication, and their usefulness in investigative interviewing were all but ignored.

Today, businesses call on private investigators to look into various offenses committed against companies or their employees. Many large businesses have trained investigators on staff to investigate crimes ranging from stalking to theft. Typically, if a Part I offense has occurred, the internal investigation is turned over to the appropriate police agency. However, if the incident can be investigated by internal security personnel, it is. Few companies want the embarrassment of a public disclosure of their problems. In addition, many businesses do not think law enforcement agencies can properly investigate so-called white-collar crimes.

In the private sector, private detectives and security personnel for corporations might investigate an incident, even though no civil or criminal matter is pending. The investigation might be aimed specifically at providing information to help management make administrative decisions regarding the violation of company rules or procedures. Often, the evidence collected never reaches the outside world or the civil or criminal courts. The decision to reveal or not reveal the evidence to the public depends on what's ultimately best for the company.

In Chapter 12, we examine internal controls and investigations from the corporate perspective and the role in which you could likely find yourself should you be working on an internal investigation.

Police agencies investigate few embezzlement cases. The vast majority of such cases are handled by private investigators. Why aren't police agencies involved in the investigation of more white-collar crimes?

Based on my 35 years of experience, I am convinced that businesses, banks in particular, do not want their internal matters revealed to the public. Reports of internal theft lead to bad press. That is, if internal losses become public knowledge, the bank's image as a safe place to deposit money will suffer.

At one time, the FBI investigated all internal and other bank thefts, and technically it still retains jurisdiction. But today the FBI does not investigate cases involving losses of only a few thousand dollars. The bureau has shifted its priorities, leaving local police agencies to investigate most cases of fraud and embezzlement. Unfortunately, local police agencies are generally not properly trained in these investigations, and even if they were, most bank managers would still prefer to handle the matter privately.

THE COLLECTION OF EVIDENCE

Whether the investigator is a police detective, a loss prevention officer of a large corporation, or a private investigator hired to look into a particular incident, he or she must operate within predefined parameters in conducting an investigation and collecting evidence. Police investigators must work within federal and state laws intended to protect society from unreasonable

police behavior. In addition, they work within the bureaucracy and operating procedures of their respective agencies. Private investigators have a
wider choice of investigative methods because there are fewer laws governing their actions. A company's internal investigators may take investigative
liberties that might seem unreasonable, but their actions do not affect society
generally. Still, their behavior is limited and controlled by company policy
and the fear of possible civil suits. Company control of an investigator's
behavior generally cannot influence the inquiry to such an extent that it
causes the investigator to violate personal ethics and professional responsibilities. If this happens, there is a question of integrity.

Regardless of whether an offense is investigated by public or private
detectives, the evidence needed to prosecute the case is the same. If a piece
of evidence is to be of value to a company (or, for that matter, to society), the
methods used to collect and preserve it must meet the highest standards
imposed by the courts. This is true even when the collected evidence serves
only to justify an employee's dismissal rather than prosecution in court. The
case may turn ugly if the fired employee sues the company for wrongful termination and the company must produce the evidence on which it based the
termination. If evidence collection and preservation fall short of acceptable
standards, the company may be in deep trouble financially. In the public
sector, of course, if a police investigator does not properly collect and preserve evidence, the prosecution's case may dissolve, allowing the guilty party
to go free.

TESTIMONIAL EVIDENCE

Obviously, the main topic of this book is the collection of testimonial evidence through investigative interviewing. Most, if not all, of the offenses
cataloged in the FBI's *Uniform Crime Report* require investigative interviewing of victims, witnesses, and suspects. Most of the evidence presented during the prosecution of Part I and Part II offenses was obtained in an interview
or interrogation.

There are legal means available to assist both public and private investigators in searching out all forms of evidence that will reveal the truth. Subpoenas, for example, help investigators collect evidence without resorting to
illegal methods.

As this book points out, the investigator's major job is to persuade the
interviewee to cooperate long enough to reveal truthful information about
the crime under investigation. To this end, investigators of all kinds must

cultivate professional attitudes and techniques that promote communication and cooperation. Most interviewees will acquiesce to requests for information, but they need encouragement from the investigator. There is always some resistance to an investigator's inquiries. Some people believe that the degree of resistance depends on the nature of the offense under investigation. My thought is that the degree of resistance is a reflection of the interviewee's personality, the interviewer's attitude, and the qualities the interviewer brings to bear on the interview.

Are people more likely to refuse to cooperate with a private investigation than with a police investigation? Certainly people perceive less of a threat from private investigations. Most consider losing a job to be less damaging than being fined or going to jail. Employees are expected to cooperate in reasonable inquiries undertaken by company management. The refusal to cooperate in an investigation is often regarded by management as insubordination and sufficient cause for dismissal. But it does not prove that the employee is guilty.

Occasionally, the greater threat of a police investigation works to obscure rather than reveal the truth. Because of the fear that a police interview can inspire, interviewees feel pressured to provide answers that they sense the investigator wants—and thus lead the police to a wrongful arrest. It can be difficult for police investigators to discover the truth while simultaneously protecting the rights of the alleged victims and the accused. There is a need for comprehensive training in interviewing at the beginning and throughout a police officer's career.

REVIEW QUESTIONS

1. How are public and private investigators alike? What is their biggest challenge?
2. What is the difference between Part I and Part II offenses in the United States? Give three examples of each.
3. How does the FBI define fraud and embezzlement?
4. Is white-collar crime a significant problem in the United States? Explain.
5. Name the various agencies that compile crime statistics in Europe.
6. What types of crimes do public investigators usually handle? What about private investigators?
7. Are police officers properly trained in the investigation of white-collar crimes? Explain.

8. Why aren't the police asked to investigate more cases of fraud, embezzlement, and internal theft?

9. Compare the responsibilities of public and private investigators in collecting and preserving evidence, and for each describe the consequences of failing to follow proper procedures.

10. How do public and private investigations differ when it comes to interviewing?

11. Why is it usually necessary for the investigator to encourage interviewees to be cooperative?

12. Are people more likely to comply with a public investigation or a private one?

CHAPTER 7

Rapport, Active Listening, and Other Techniques

Rapport is the understanding between individuals created by genuine interest and concern.

—*Karen M. Hess and Wayne W. Bennett,* **Criminal Investigation** *(1991)*

The interviewing process is not limited to the criminal justice and security arena. Interviews are conducted in virtually every area of human endeavor. Human resource specialists conduct interviews routinely; supervisors conduct them routinely as they conduct performance plans and handle disciplinary problems. Doctors, lawyers, admission coordinators, pastors—all perform interviews as one of their many job responsibilities. During any interview, no matter whom is the interviewer or for whatever reason the interview is being conducted, the interviewer needs to build rapport along with being proficient in active listening.

Interviews are not normal social encounters in which two people exchange ideas and experiences on an equal footing. In an investigative interview, the interviewee should do most of the talking while the investigator acts as a catalyst, a persuader, and a stimulator of thoughts. The catalyst promotes an unspoken chemistry that produces cooperation. He or she asks appropriate questions to probe for facts, anecdotes, and feelings from the interviewee. To prepare for your role as interviewer-catalyst, look at each inquiry with clear thinking as you plan your approach. Detach yourself from the emotional content of the interview, adopt a positive attitude, and be flexible. In your role as catalyst, two basic interviewing tactics will prove useful: building rapport and active listening. We will look at each technique in turn.

BUILDING RAPPORT

Mutual confidence and trust are difficult to establish in an interview, and the interviewee is not always your partner in seeking the truth. Your goal is to determine the truth in an investigation; the interviewee's goal might be to protect himself from a variety of consequences. You can overcome this obstacle and encourage interviewees to provide information by building *rapport*. If you can plan, organize, and evoke cooperation in social situations, you probably possess basic qualities of leadership and can establish rapport, inspire confidence, elicit information, and keep interviews under control.

Rapport can be described as a good feeling or warmth that exists between people and is characterized by an interpersonal relationship that is cooperative. In an interview, rapport is like an electric current that flows between participants. It is based on how they communicate rather than on what they say, and it requires practiced effort. Rapport involves building a degree of comfortableness together and a level of trust in one another. It is basic goodwill that permits nondefensive behavior. To develop rapport is to create a feeling within yourself and the interviewee of alertness, well-being, and even excitement. Rapport is a psychological closeness established in the very beginning of an interview, when you blend your verbal and nonverbal actions with those of the interviewee. The first few minutes are crucial because people determine their basic impressions of one another during the first few minutes of an interview. Rapport is important in an interview because the degree of rapport you establish determines the degree of compliance you obtain from the interviewee.

Investigators who succeed in establishing rapport with interviewees demonstrate their empathy with them and generally obtain their truthful cooperation. They feel less inhibited in asking questions, even questions about sensitive or personal matters, and interviewees are less resistant about answering. The development of rapport does not require that the interviewer become emotionally involved or that the interviewer's commitment, persistence, or objectivity be eroded. You are not trying to become the interviewee's best buddy. You are trying to solve the case. You want the interviewee to buy into your friendliness only long enough so that you can obtain the information you need. When all is said and done, no one will misunderstand your behavior.

Active listening, discussed later in this chapter, is an important technique for building rapport, but there are others. Rapport can be developed through small talk, a good orientation, and through a very warm, friendly manner. To achieve rapport with the interviewee, try to find an area of common interest. There is usually something that you can find that could help identify with the interviewee. You can call attention to similarities in such subtle ways as by complimenting the person (thus showing that you have similar tastes).[1] You can also build rapport by enhancing the interviewee's self-image. If your inquiry is handled in a professional way so that

---

[1] Downs, et al., 1980, p. 259; Nierenberg, 1968.

cooperation will benefit the interviewee's self-image, he or she will feel honored to cooperate and will later be proud of assisting "the authorities." Attempt to make your inquiry relevant to the interviewee's life and concerns. Your attitude is communicated by the ways you listen and ask questions. People find it flattering to be asked for their opinions. In an interview, this technique compliments the interviewee's views and may strengthen rapport. Expressions of genuine interest and empathy, positive recognition, easy eye contact, and appropriate positive silences also help build and maintain rapport.

At the beginning of an interaction, the interviewee may display signs of uneasiness. Even truthful interviewees may have some anxiety over whether you will be fair and unbiased in your methods and judgment. As rapport develops, you may notice a distinct sigh of relief, signaling a lessening of the interviewee's distress and the building of trust. From that point onward, the interview may take on a more relaxed character.

You need to be alert to whether the interviewee is truly listening. Just because interviewees are silent and appear to be listening does not mean that they are truly receptive to what you are saying. They may be lost in an emotional maze of fear. Periodically ask questions designed to test whether the interviewee is listening. A blank, unresponsive stare may signal distress, unclear thinking, or an unbalanced mental process.

Control your emotions without losing your enthusiasm. Keep your thoughts collected and composed; think your comments through carefully before presenting them to the interviewee. Refuse to become ruffled, and keep your goal clearly in mind. The use of sarcasm, ridicule, or cynicism only creates tension instead of building rapport and gaining cooperation from the interviewee. Generally speaking, people resist being thought of as inferior and might be reluctant to establish rapport with or to be persuaded by anyone who tries, either consciously or unconsciously, to make them feel that way. Instead, help the interviewee rationalize and save face. Other actions that tend to block rapport are making negative comments, engaging in monologues, second-guessing the interviewee, displaying a condescending attitude, and trying to hurry through the interview.[2]

Through participant role reversal, an interviewee may skillfully unseat you and take over the role of leader in the interview. An inexperienced interviewer may not see the signals of this switchover and may discover too late that he or she has given up command of the interview, answering

---

[2] Downs, et al., 1980, p. 201; Bennis, et al., 973, p. 199.

rather than asking questions. This role reversal is embarrassing only if it continues. Proficient interviewers realize when role reversal is taking place and immediately regain control without making it too obvious or causing conflict. Entering into a power struggle with interviewees can create alienation instead of rapport.

When you're ending an unsuccessful interview, do nothing to create hard feelings. Even when hostile interviewees refuse to answer your questions, don't hold a grudge; don't show disgust, frustration, or anger; and don't allow yourself to vent your displeasure. Don't allow your pride to cause you to blame interviewees for their lack of cooperation. Instead, lay a positive foundation for future interviews. Aim to have all interviewees leave with a positive feeling, allowing them to believe that they experienced a meaningful and valuable interaction.

ACTIVE LISTENING

There are two main conditions of listening: the passive (inattentive) and the active (attentive). Most of us are good at passive listening. We appear to be listening when, in fact, our minds have wandered off. Too often, our need to talk is greater than our ability to listen.

To become an effective interviewer, you should practice to become a better listener. A good interviewer has usually practiced and developed the skill of being a good listener. By staying keenly aware of the important role of active listening in an interview, you can analyze and encourage in a meaningful way. You can use active listening skills to determine the interviewee's frame of reference and to reduce emotional tension. Rely on your spontaneity, sensitivity, and basic common sense; listen better and understand more. Avoid putting on a show of authority, displaying more interest in yourself and your role than in listening to the interviewee.

Most people feel that no one really listens to them. Your interviewees will appreciate the opportunity to show their knowledge and to express their ideas and feelings. They hunger for that feeling of importance they get from being asked for their views.

The first step in empathizing is to listen and attempt to grasp the meaning of what is said. Your effort to listen actively demonstrates your recognition of the interviewee's worth and encourages continued cooperation. Active listening involves your total person and must be a part of your presentation. You can exhibit your attentiveness to the interviewee through the intonation of your voice, the positioning of your body, and your facial expressions.

Through questioning, paraphrasing, rephrasing, and reflecting, you will show the interviewee that you are listening. The important tactic of active listening requires attentiveness and concentration, acceptance, detachment, and patience. We discuss each of these qualities before exploring in more detail how you, the interviewer, can signal active listening.

Attentiveness and Concentration

With a little effort, you can learn to be a skilled listener. Being alert and courteous, giving the interviewee your undivided attention, and being prepared with appropriate questions or comments show that you are interested in what the interviewee says. The benefits of such attentiveness are numerous. There is a close connection between active listening and intuition; active listening helps you sense meanings that are not revealed in words alone. The development of rapport is built on a foundation that is partly made up of your ability to show that you are listening. Your attentiveness implies acceptance and encourages the interviewee to say more. It allows the interviewee to sense the genuine, unplanned, spontaneous you. In the end, being attentive to the interviewee helps you achieve your ultimate goal: gathering truthful information.

Give the interviewee your full attention. Ponder, at least momentarily, each of the interviewee's comments. People can sense if you are truly interested by the subtle way you pause to reflect on what they say. As an active listener, you should be able to control unnecessary distractions. Avoid an indifferent attitude. One way of turning people off is to not pay attention to their comments or to be thinking of the next question to ask and not paying total attention to the interviewee. Preoccupied glances, slack body posture, and inappropriate silences and comments all imply boredom. Inattentive listeners do not truly hear what is being said; they superficially signal hearing and responding, but no real thoughts are formulated. They are a bit out of rhythm with the conversation and the mood of the interaction. In a fast-moving interview, they fail to provide sharp, alert, quick responses.

People can sense when you are preoccupied, bored, or inattentive. Interviewees who sense that you are bored or that your interest is not genuine may feel used by you. When facing an inattentive listener, these interviewees tend to regard the interaction as a waste of time and may hold back information. Because they may not outwardly express their reasons for withdrawing, you might never realize that *your* inattention stopped the flow of information.

Active listening means concentrating on everything said and not said, both verbally and nonverbally. Evaluate the interviewee's subjective comments in light of his emotional state, attitudes, and values. Use all your skills to analyze the story he tells you. Try to determine the interviewee's frame of reference and what might have led him there. Evaluating interviewees properly helps you determine how hurriedly you can conduct the interview and what direction it should take. Interviewees who feel rushed may sense that you are insincere in your efforts and may discourage them from being cooperative. Always be alert for signals of the interviewee's mental processes, and look for clues of motivation and hidden needs. As you listen to what the interviewee has to say, continually observe the way he acts. Through mannerisms, gestures, recurrent phrases, and modes of expression, interviewees signal their thinking, their hidden needs, and possible deception. Avoid idle thinking by concentrating on the specifics of the interview. Listen constructively to the interviewee, and more important, *concentrate!*

Some inexperienced interviewers are so busy thinking of their next question that they forget to listen to the interviewee's answers. Deceitful interviewees can take advantage of the investigator's inattention by making innocuous comments or failing to fully answer questions. If you don't concentrate, deceptive interviewees with moderate skills can easily mislead you. Even evasive interviewees, who are not really deceptive but only reluctant or hesitant to comply, can mislead you. Some interviewees like the challenge of testing interviewers, which is why being in control of the interview and paying attention are so critical.

Acceptance

The listener who exhibits nonjudgmental understanding and who provides empathic responses encourages others to continue to communicate. By actively listening to interviewees, you signal your acceptance of them, and they intuitively sense that it is okay to talk to you. Empathize with their attitudes, the roles they are playing, and their expressed and demonstrated needs.

Like most people, interviewees often think that what they have to say is the most important thing in the world, and they continually evaluate their listeners. If you are receptive, understanding, warm, responsive, interested, and involved, interviewees will probably enter into a dialogue with you. They will be responsive in a productive, permissive atmosphere. Although interviewees expect and appreciate appropriate responses to their comments, they don't necessarily seek an evaluation. They need reassurance, support, and acceptance while revealing their thoughts and exposing their secrets. Recognizing the interviewee's dignity, worth, and importance will help improve the productivity of the interview. By appearing to be helpful and maintaining a friendly attitude, the interviewee will be more likely to cooperate.

The ideal interviewer listens with nonjudgmental understanding and does not criticize or bully. By exhibiting genuine interest, you can avoid injecting your opinions, value judgments, and criticisms into the interview. When interviewees sense that you are evaluating them with your personal set of values, they may become defensive, which will curtail the flow of information. Try to maintain a universal set of values as well as your personal set of values. Neatly tuck your personal values away when you interview. Maintain the attitude that no behavior is too aggressive, no feeling too guilty or shameful, for the interviewee to bring into the interview.

Use sounds and actions to signal your acceptance of the interviewee. Murmur vocal sounds like "Uh-huh" at appropriate times during the interview. Using facial expressions and gestures will let the interviewee know you are listening and being attentive. If the interviewee talks spontaneously, avoid interrupting them until there is a significant pause. Encourage the interviewee to continue by nodding your head and continuing to listen attentively.

Detachment

Occasionally you might need to investigate crimes that are so horrible that they shake you to your very core or turn your stomach. As you investigate crimes that would make most people angry or sick, you might have to take control of your emotions and hide feelings of outrage. When you are expected to remain calm and listen, your body cannot vent the pent-up pressure caused by stress. No matter what the circumstances, don't be thrown off balance. Don't become so angry that you want to seek revenge on behalf of the victim. Remain detached and gain the interviewee's cooperation by treating him or her with some level of human dignity. Being somewhat depersonalized helps the interviewer react with calm acceptance toward the interviewee.

Be secure in your personal identity. Understand yourself and maintain a sturdy philosophical core around your personal and cultural values. When interviewees respond to your questions in an angry outburst, detach yourself. Don't react in a defensive, defiant manner. You might say, "I see your point of view" or "I understand what you mean." You will only alienate the interviewee if you react emotionally. Making threats and insults does not do much for your professionalism and will only make the interviewee less cooperative.

Patience

Inexperienced interviewers often rush from one question to another without waiting for an answer. Experienced interviewers understand that patience is a necessary component of active listening. Impatience signals ridicule, cynicism, and intimidation on the part of the interviewer and blocks rapport. Impatience toward interviewees is self-defeating and can only be characterized as abusive and judgmental. Rather than use rapid-fire questioning, proficient interviewers allow interviewees time to answer fully without interruption, thereby showing interest and attentiveness. By speaking softly, slowly, and firmly, they signal that they are capable of both comprehending and solving the investigative problem. With composure, serenity, and emotional strength, they advance toward their goal. That calmness and strength are patience at work.

To be a good listener, after you ask a question, you should be quiet and stay patient until the interviewee talks. As they talk, interviewees generally begin to feel comfortable enough to reveal the information you need. Avoid interrupting or making unnecessary comments; the most important role you have is to remain totally attentive. It is through times of tension that interviewees test your sincerity. Your patience in an interview signals tolerance, acceptance, and understanding while it stimulates dialogue. Patience carries with it forgiveness and respect for interviewees. Painstakingly and patiently advance, point by point and item by item, toward your goal. If the interviewee becomes hostile or indignant, try to remain calm and work toward cooperation. The key is to be patient and persistent. Do not rebuff the interviewee. As Benjamin Disraeli, the 19th-century British prime minister, said, "Next to knowing when to seize an advantage, the most important thing in life is to know when to forego an advantage."

Your patience is vital in the face of an emotional outburst. A sensitive response to a victim or witness in distress is essential in reducing the person's fear. Permit interviewees to discharge their stored anger or pain in an emotional dumping process. Listen to interviewees as though you think they have something worthwhile to offer. The interviewee may test the degree of your patience by making irrelevant conversation. The strength of your gentleness, patience, and kindness leads to confidence in your judgment.

Be alert to both concrete and abstract information. Concrete, objective explanations paint a clear picture of the event or situation. Abstract, subjective comments are emotional, nonspecific, and often misleading. Strive to obtain concrete information, but accept that the interviewee will also express emotion and make many subjective comments.

As your career progresses, you will come in contact with many different personality types. Some interviewees are impulsive, egotistical, and childish, with a low tolerance for frustration. Others are better at controlling their impulses and will seek to collaborate with you to solve the crime. Your patience can guide the inquiry, no matter what personality type you need to interview.

SIGNALING ACTIVE LISTENING

Although verbal communication is the most distinctive of human achievements, nonverbal communication, including body language, touch, and positive silence, is equally important. Feelings and intentions are conveyed through body posture and movement, gestures, facial expressions, and eye contact. In fact, expectations are conveyed mostly through nonverbal communication. Nonverbal communication, which is learned throughout life, reveals underlying personality traits, subconscious attitudes, intentions, and conflicts. Use it to your advantage in an interview. Express your willingness to listen to the interviewee by engaging your whole body in the communication process and not merely your words. Move forward in your chair, nod your head, wear a curious expression, and smile to encourage the interviewee to continue speaking. Some interviewers are highly skilled in the use of nonverbal communication. Others can learn how to use body language, touch, and positive silence to express their positive expectations and willingness to listen.

Body Language

Body language includes posture, movement, gestures, facial expression, and eye contact. It is an important part of the climate of an interview, which is in play from the beginning to the end of the encounter. You will convey your expectations to the interviewee through your body language. During an interview, your nonverbal behavior is under constant scrutiny, and a single negative message has the potential to render an entire interview ineffective.

Before you utter your first word, the interviewee will examine you for signs of acceptance and trustworthiness. Your only defense is to display positive and believable signals of acceptance. A subtle delivery is needed to avoid the appearance of pretense and to avoid arousing the interviewee's suspicion. Use your tone of voice, deliberate silences, and variations in eye contact, facial expressions, distancing, and posture to express positive or negative feelings.

Body Posture and Movement

Signal that you are paying attention to the interviewee by sharing postures, by standing or sitting close, and by facing the interviewee squarely or at a 45-degree angle. Move slowly and confidently to avoid scaring the interviewee. Lean forward to show that you are warm and attentive. When you disagree with something the interviewee has said, be careful not to allow your posture or movement to announce your disagreement. People generally shift their position before voicing their disagreement with what the speaker has said.

When you sense that you are communicating effectively with an interviewee, some nonverbal movement in synchrony with the interviewee will signaling attentive listening. Try to move in time to the rhythm of the speaker. People are drawn to those who seem to mirror them. Just as a perfect meshing of gears is essential to a smooth-running engine, an effective meshing of personalities is a key to a successful interview.

Gestures, Facial Expression, and Tone of Voice

Proficient investigators use nonconfrontational interviewing tactics, and their body language reflects a nonconfrontational style. If your gestures are in any way accusatory—for example, pointing your finger—the interviewee will become defensive and likely will shut down. When gesturing, display your total involvement in what is being said. Keep your arms open and your palms extended. Turn your head toward the interviewee; do not look at him or her out of the corner of your eye. Look at the interviewee often, and wear an interested or pleased expression. Your face will not crack and break if you flex your facial muscles to show expression! Be careful not to indicate an authoritarian attitude with your facial expressions or intonation, though. Responding with phrases such as "I see," "Please go on," and "Uh- huh" will show that you are interested and they should continue talking. But the impact of these phrases can be negative or positive depending on how they are expressed. You might say, "Please go on," but stop the flow of information with a tone that proclaims disbelief or boredom. Collect evidence in a fair and impartial manner by keeping your tone alert and neutral.

Eye Contact

The interviewer's easy eye contact promotes rapport with the interviewee and encourages communication. Like gestures, eye contact works to control the flow of conversation. It is common for interviewers to look away for a few seconds before they finish speaking and then to look back as they are continue. Used properly, eye contact is effective in establishing and maintaining communication.

If you are a dominant, assertive individual, be careful how you use eye contact. You don't want to frighten interviewees with your eye contact pattern. Do not stare at the interviewee; this creates undue stress, which can interfere with communication. Be sure to give the interviewee time to think clearly and talk. Through continued practice, you will know the right time to talk and the right time to listen.

Touch

Touching another human being in a gentle, reassuring way indicates concern, warmth, and closeness. At times it is helpful to place your hand gently on the interviewee's hand, arm, or shoulder. A reassuring touch strengthens the bonds of rapport. Proficient interviewers learn to use reassuring touch to exhibit their acceptance of the interviewee and to strengthen interpersonal communication. When it seems fitting, your touch can be an integral part of an interview, signaling a special caring that is inexpressible through words.

A complicated combination of things occurs when two people touch, however, so be careful to determine whether it is appropriate to touch a particular interviewee. Not everyone will allow touching to take place. Hostile or extremely reluctant interviewees will usually not allow themselves to be touched—sometimes not even to shake hands. Many interviewees sense their personal space as an extension of their ego and will go to almost any length to preserve it. They do not want others to come close to them, and they certainly do not want to be touched by anyone. This restraint usually has nothing to do with you personally and probably has nothing to do with the matter under investigation.

Positive Silence

The tactic of silence can be a weapon for battle or a marvelous instrument of the most delicate construction. Improperly used, the interviewer's silence is a form of authoritarian punishment. The use of abusive silence is a self-defeating tactic that often offends the interviewee, builds tension, and discourages cooperation. Unless employed subtly, your silence may be equated with withdrawal, rejection, disapproval, or an implied threat. Silence shakes up interviewees when it occurs repeatedly.

When used appropriately, however, without an intentional threat to the interviewee, silence can strengthen rapport and encourage compliance. You can use a positive silence to indicate your acceptance of the interviewee or to signal your control of the interview. Interviewees can sense the mood of the moment, the implicit meaning of the interviewer's silence. I support using silence to keep the pot bubbling but not to antagonize or alienate interviewees. It can be a constructive part of your tactics and need not be a harsh method.

Keep your questions simple and direct, and wait after asking each question, to give the interviewee time to reply. A brief silence or pause after the interviewee finishes speaking can be used to indicate that more is expected in response to the question. When you pause between questions, sometimes interviewees provide further information to fill the silence. A positive silence can produce meaningful and relevant information that might not otherwise be provided. Research indicates that there is positive correlation between the amount of silence used by the interviewer and the interviewee's general level of spontaneity.[3] When I choose to use silence as a tactic, I glance at the interviewee rather than stare. Staring can be oppressive when coupled with silence; silence alone is enough to bring out meaningful tension in the interviewee. It is sometimes helpful to introduce silence when the interviewee least expects it.

As useful a tactic as positive silence is, some interviewees can withstand it. Experienced, composed interviewees handle silence by sitting patiently and expectantly or by asking questions to distract you from your efforts. Some interviewees handle silence by returning the interviewer's stare with a calm, anticipatory look. Others counter with their own silence in hopes of revealing the interviewer's tension or lack of confidence. Interviewees' skill in handling silence is a sign of their ability to control distress. Hence, it is beneficial to try to gauge an interviewee's skill in this regard.

---

[3] Gordon, 1969, p. 188; Dexter, 1970, p. 112.

Interviewees who resent authority might have long intervals of silence before answering your questions. Interviewees who have a poor self-image, who feel inadequate and helpless, may use silence to express their annoyance, resentment, or anger. They may engage in lengthy pauses, sudden silences, and an unexplained inability to discuss pertinent details.[4] Many interviewees resent being interrupted when speaking. Some can become so petulant, impatient, or irritable that they refuse to talk at all. Interviewees who realize that silence makes the questioner uncomfortable may intentionally use it to antagonize the interviewer and may decide to *stay* silent.

Inexperienced interviewers sometimes have a low tolerance for silence and become distressed by it. For anxious interviewers who lack self-confidence, a brief period of silence may seem almost endless. However, the interviewee's silence is not necessarily a deterrent, and it need not disrupt the interviewer's strategy. Through training and practice, interviewers can learn to tolerate quiet in an interview and to use it to maximum advantage. Even if the interviewee's silence makes you feel uneasy, opposed, or thwarted, it is vital that you not respond in an aggressive manner. Remember that this is an interview with someone who probably doesn't want to talk to you, so don't take things, including silence, personally, since it is not a personal attack. It is equally important that you not suggest responses to your questions. When I sense that interviewees are trying to use silence to their advantage, I assume that they are also using other ploys to try to manipulate me. These formidable competitors need special attention, closer observation, and more careful assessment. Truthful, straightforward, compliant interviewees do not employ tactics of strategic silence.

Remember that building rapport is a skill that can be learned by practicing. If proper rapport is established, you should be successful in obtaining the information you are seeking.

REVIEW QUESTIONS

1. How does the interviewer act as a catalyst during an interview?
2. What is rapport?
3. When should you begin to develop rapport during an interview?
4. What are the advantages of establishing rapport?
5. Are you approving of the crime when you are friendly to the criminal?
6. How might you go about building rapport?

[4] Woody and Woody, 1972, p. 163; Drake, 1972, p. 86.

7. How can you tell if a silent interviewee is truly listening?
8. Why doesn't the use of sarcasm, ridicule, or cynicism help you gain cooperation?
9. What is role reversal, and how should it be handled?
10. How should you end an unproductive interview?
11. What is active listening?
12. What does it take to be a "perfect listener"?
13. How can you show that you are paying attention to the interviewee?
14. What are the consequences of inattention during an interview?
15. Why is it important to concentrate during an interview?
16. How can you signal your acceptance of the interviewee?
17. What is detachment, and how can you use it?
18. Why is patience a virtue for interviewers?
19. How can you use body language to signal positive messages?
20. How does eye contact help control the flow of conversation?
21. When is it okay to touch an interviewee?
22. How can you use silence in positive ways?
23. How *shouldn't* you respond to an interviewee's silence?

CHAPTER 8

Authority

SECURITY'S PLACE IN THE ORGANIZATION[1]

The degree and nature of the authority vested in security management and investigations become matters of the greatest importance when such a function is fully integrated into the organization. Any evaluation of the scope and authority required by security investigations to perform effectively must consider a variety of factors, both formal and informal, that exist in the structure. Here we examine these factors.

Definition of Authority

It is management's responsibility to establish the level of authority on which security may operate in order to accomplish its mission. Security must have authority to deal with the establishment of security systems. It must be able to conduct inspections of performance in many areas of the company. It must be in a position to evaluate performance and risk throughout the company.

All such authority relationships, of course, should be clearly established by management and made with the assistance and guidance of a professional consultant. This trend has caused a growth in the number of security consultants, particularly independent consultants who do not have a vested interest in the outcome of their recommendations.

Determining costs and effectiveness is only the first step. Having done this, management will then have to face the important question of whether security can be truly and totally integrated into the organization. If, upon analysis, it is found that the existing structure would in some way suffer from the addition of new organizational functions, alternatives to the integrated proprietary security department must be sought. These alternatives usually consist only of the application and supervision of physical security measures. This inevitably results in the fragmentation of protective systems in the various areas requiring security. However, these alternatives are sometimes effective, especially in those firms whose overall risk and vulnerability are low. But as the crime rates continue to climb and as criminal methods of

[1] Gion Green, *Introduction to Security*, 4th ed., Butterworth-Heinemann, 1987.

attack and the underground network of distribution continue to become more sophisticated, anything less than total integration will become increasingly inadequate.

Once management has recognized that existing problems—real or potential—make the introduction or enlargement of security a necessity for continued effective operation, it is obliged to exert every effort to create an atmosphere in which security can exert its full efforts to accomplish stated company objectives. Any equivocation by management at this point can only serve to weaken or ultimately undermine the security effectiveness that might be obtained by a clearer statement of total support and directives resulting in intra-company cooperation with security efforts.

Levels of Authority

Obviously security managers operate at many mixtures of authority levels. Their functional authority may encompass a relatively limited area, prescribed by broad outlines of basic company policy. In matters of investigation, they may be limited to a staff function in which they may advise and recommend or even assist in conducting the investigation but not have direct control over or even assist in conducting the investigation, and they would not have direct control or command over the routines of employees.

It is customary for security managers to exercise line authority over preventive activities of the company. In this situation, they command the guards, who in turn command the employees in all matters over which security managers have jurisdiction. Security managers, of course, have full line authority over the conduct of their own departments, within which they too have staff personnel as well as those to whom they have delegated functional authority.

The Power of Security Personnel

Security personnel are generally limited to the exercise of powers possessed by every citizen. There is no legal area in which the position of a security office as such confers greater rights, powers, or privileges than those possessed by every citizen. A few states—for example, Michigan—confer additional arrest powers for security personnel after the completion of 135 hours of training. As a practical matter, if the security officer is uniformed, he will very likely find that in most cases people will comply with his requests. Many people are not aware of their own rights or of the limitations of powers of a security officer. Thus a security officer can obtain compliance to directives that, if not illegal, at least may be beyond his or her power to command. This acquiescence is usually harmless, but in cases where a security officer has unwisely taken liberties with his authority, the officer and the officer's employer are subject to the penalties of a tort action. The litigation involved in suing a security officer and his employer for tortious conduct is slow and expensive, which may make such recourse impossible for the poor and those unfamiliar with their rights. But the judgments that have been awarded have had a generally sobering effect on security professionals and have probably served to reduce the number of such incidents.

Criminal law also regulates security activities. Major crimes such as battery, manslaughter, kidnapping, and breaking and entering—any one of which may be confronted in the course of security activities—are substantially deterred by criminal sanctions.

Further limitations may be imposed on the authority of a security force by licensing laws, administrative regulations, and specific statues directed at security activities. Operating contracts between employers and security firms may also specify limits on the activities of the contracted personnel.

Authority and Neutrality in the Investigative Interview

Typically, an authority figure functions as a representative of some organization or entity. As difficult as it may seem, an investigator is most successful when maintaining a middle ground, balancing on the tightrope of neutrality. An investigator's loyalty is to the organization she represents, but it can be extremely helpful to the success of an inquiry if this connection is obscured and not too clearly discernible.

AUTHORITY AND POWER

In its simplest form, *power* is the ability to control, influence, or causes other to do what you want them to do.[2] Power can be expressed negatively or positively. *Authority* is the vested or conveyed right to exercise power over others. It is the right to command, to enforce laws, to exact obedience, to determine, or to judge, and its basis may be legal, traditional, or social. Investigators wield the authority granted them by virtue of their position, and they function on behalf of a segment of the community.[3] As with all positions of authority, an organization establishes guidelines that impact

[2] Effective Uses of Power and Authority, 1980.
[3] Bennis et al., 1973, p. 62.

investigators' behavior. Each investigator then functions based on personal ethics, and no matter which organization investigators represent, they are personally responsible for how they command, determine avenues of inquiry, and judge outcomes. Because the misuse of their authority carries serious potential consequences, investigators have a great responsibility to exercise their power thoughtfully.

Some investigators wrongly consider power to be a permanent possession. In fact, legitimate power emanates from the role or position that the investigator holds. When used positively in an interview, authority promotes confidence and accomplishment, boosting the interviewee's self-esteem and encouraging his cooperation.

Liability Concerns for Investigators

Anyone can be sued for anything. However, many investigators who cross the invisible line may face liability. Here are several situations that might cause liability concerns:

- Conducting applicant background checks
- Not conducting applicant background checks
- Detaining and interrogating employees
- Search and seizure in the workplace
- Undercover and surveillance operations
- Employee discharge and failure to discharge
- Disclosing evidence in worker's compensation and unemployment hearings
- Obtaining information illegally
- Misrepresentation and failure to warn about ex-employees
- Filing criminal charges
- Discrimination-based investigations
- Union and nonunion member investigations
- False acquisition based on sloppy investigation
- Misuse of wiretap
- Abuse of authority
- Abuse of power
- Filing or claiming false charges
- Failure to follow legal process to get IP address
- Suing for fraud
- Being an unlicensed investigator and providing a service
- Carrying a gun to work

- Withholding evidence
- Spreading unfounded slander
- Releasing confidential information

The Misuse of Authority

Some interviewers exercise their authority aggressively all the time rather than assertively and only when necessary. These authoritarians demand absolute obedience without regard for the individual rights of others.[4] When crossed, they become intolerant. They threaten interviewees, describing the steps they will take if the interviewee does not cooperate. Arrogantly passing judgment, authoritarians humiliate interviewees, stripping them of their self-respect. They expect to be treated like gods, and they often are, because of the lack of awareness of their real selves. They are corrupt, prejudiced, sadistic opportunists exploiting their positions of power to try to earn the respect of their peers.

Authoritarians wield their power in such a way as to make interviewees feel helpless, impotent, and fearful, forcing them on the defensive.[5] The investigator's superior attitude tells interviewees that the investigator is not seeking a problem-solving relationship, that their help is not desired, and that it is likely that their power, status, or worth will be reduced if they cooperate with the investigation.[6] The result is resistance. If the investigator responds aggressively to resistance, someone may get hurt. The modulated use of power is the only legal and civilized tactic.

The more you understand about what is happening in the interview, the more likely it is that you will respond in a constructive manner.[7] We all act in accordance with our own individual reasoning power; we tend to invent plausible explanations or rationalizations for our actions.[8] Typically, interviewees use rationalization to preserve their self-image.[9] Your use of power in any form may provoke the interviewee to behave defensively.[10] Anxiety does not promote compliance. Therefore, avoid entering into a power struggle with interviewees; this will only lead to alienation.[11]

[4] Bennis et al., 1973.
[5] Bennis et al., 1973, p. 252.
[6] Bennis et al., 1973, p. 492.
[7] OSS Assessment Staff, 1948, p. 171.
[8] Nierenberg, 1968.
[9] Berg and Bass, 1961, p. 252.
[10] Woody and Woody, 1972, p. 170.
[11] Nirenberg, 1963.

The Positive Application of Authority

The authoritarian interviewer's negative use of power arises from his feelings of insecurity and inadequacy. Proficient interviewers, on the other hand, use power in positive ways as they strive toward personal growth and self-affirmation. They are empowered with self-appreciation, vision, and purpose. Personal motivation is based on the principle that you are the end result of what you want to be. Success comes from inner strength, conscious will-power, and an unwavering determination to succeed. With these you can develop courage, enthusiasm, confidence, and belief in your own ability.

When the needs of interview participants clash, develop a strategy to use to your advantage, applying referent power, the power of your position that symbolizes the organization you work for, in subtle ways. To argue with the interviewee is self-defeating, as is running away. For interviewees, information is power. Faced with a threatening authoritarian, interviewees rarely see any constructive advantage to giving up what little power they retain. You should be willing to subtly and indirectly reach a point of agreement where some of the interviewee's needs are met. Interviewees may willingly provide information in return for assurances of confidentiality, protection, or some other concession.

Interviewees who have been pushed, pressured, bribed, or overpowered by parents or other authority figures may be guarded, extremely uncomfortable, or uncooperative during an interview. Don't take the interviewee's resistance personally. You may merely be a handy authority figure for the interviewee to lash out at. Try to subtly suggest that power returns to those who decide to comply.

The interviewing techniques suggested in this book are intended to encourage your use of positive authority in everything you do—from the tone of your voice to the way you actively listen. Although you may to some degree be insecure and self-consciousness in your behavior, your human interaction skills will improve with practice. It is too easy to use harsh, abrasive methods. If you strengthen your willpower, you will not be easily drawn into destructive behavior.

NEUTRALITY

True professionals never collect evidence to suit some preconceived notion of who is culpable. To be a successful interviewer, you should approach all investigations (and all interviewees) with a floating-point strategy and an open mind. Collect all available evidence fairly and impartially, and allow it to lead you to a logical conclusion.

Encourage the interviewee's compliance by deliberately establishing your neutrality.[12] Keep all your remarks neutral, avoiding a critical or judgmental stance.[13] You might even give the impression that you are ever so slightly leaning toward the interviewee's side. It is important to demonstrate respect for all interviewees and an awareness of their need for security.[14] Interview subjects can generally tell your "party line" by your opening words.[15] It takes but a few moments, a few words, a few nonverbal signals to reveal your relative position—that is, your opinion of the interviewee. A biased or judgmental demeanor may adversely affect the outcome of the interview and may limit your investigative progress.[16] Do not conduct the interview in an accusatory way; instead, keep yourself open, positive, and neutral. Do not reveal any suspicions you might have of the interviewee's truthfulness or innocence until and if the time is right to do so. Especially when you want someone to undergo a detection-of-deception exam or other test, it is important to adopt a neutral, wait-and-see stance. The tension associated with the test may be enough to interfere with the interviewee's clear thinking, causing him to refuse to cooperate. Don't make matters worse by taking on an accusatory attitude.

While remaining neutral and objective in your methods, do not give interviewees a way of relieving tensions easily except through verbal expression. Encourage them to evaluate their situation on its real merits rather than be guided by anxiety, irritation, or other emotions.[17] Criminal victims and witnesses may allow their feelings and emotions to cloud the facts, distorting the information you seek. Do your best to lead interviewees from emotional responses to factual responses based on clear thinking.[18]

Do not allow the interviewee's mood to determine your mood or composure. Be prepared to put up with a certain amount of verbal abuse from rebellious interviewees. Your neutral stance in explaining how the interviewee can assist in your inquiry is vital to your success.

[12] Dexter, 1970, p. 25.
[13] Kahn and Cannell, 1957.
[14] Kahn and Cannell, 1957, p. 126.
[15] Bennis et al., 1973, p. 490.
[16] Dexter, 1970, p. 150.
[17] Nirenberg, 1963.
[18] Maltz, 1960.

Signaling Your Neutrality

Interviewees can pick up on subtle signals that belie your claims of neutrality. It is nearly impossible for interviewers to eliminate the effects of prejudice, hate, and other emotions on their behavior. However, investigators can control the expression of their personal views and values to avoid destroying their chances of obtaining an interviewee's compliance.

Presenting a neutral facade is a difficult task. Regardless of the hat you wear, interviewees may suspect some hidden objective or ulterior motive. Hence you should do your best to avoid displaying negative signals during an interview. Many comments can be negative or positive in character, depending on how they are voiced. Saying "Uh-huh" or "Right" with the wrong intonation might stop the flow of information. Your tone of voice may signal that you are biased, not neutral, causing a breakdown in communication.

Your tone of voice, facial expressions, language, and timing must all be congruent with your claim of neutrality. If by force, volume, or tone of voice you emphasize certain consequences, the interviewee will quickly decide that you're hoping to hear a particular response. Consequences imply an either-or situation, such as, "If you don't do such and such, then . . . ." If you repeatedly call attention to a particular set of consequences or if you react to an interviewee's focus on the positive consequences by quickly switching to a discussion of the negative consequences, the interviewee may question your neutrality.

Making an Accusation

Why would an interviewee talk openly with an investigator who seems judgmental, critical, or skeptical? You will find that it is difficult to keep your personal views and your suspicions hidden, but doing so is vital to the progress of your inquiry. Don't be too quick to provide an opinion regarding the interviewee's veracity. Don't make your suspicions known until you are reasonably certain of your facts. Interviewees who sense that you have prematurely concluded that they're lying will become defensive. When you have been convinced, after analyzing all the evidence, then your personal views may be more evident. Reserve your opinion until then.

REVIEW QUESTIONS

1. Define the terms *power* and *authority*.
2. Why must investigators exercise their power thoughtfully?

3. Describe some tactics used by authoritarians.
4. What message does the investigator's superior attitude send to the interviewee?
5. What does information represent to the interviewee, and why might he or she be reluctant to share it?
6. Why do some people resist authority?
7. Is it possible for the investigator to hold all the power in an interview? If so, would this be a good idea? Explain.
8. Name five liability concerns for investigators.
9. Why should investigators keep an open mind when they're beginning an investigation?
10. How can investigators adopt a neutral attitude?
11. How can the investigator avoid displaying negative nonverbal signals during an interview?

CHAPTER 9

Overview of the Interview Process

In this chapter, we will review the different stages of the interview process and learn how to apply some of the tactical concepts discussed earlier in this book. You are encouraged to use these tactics to think about interviewing in new ways. There is an interplay among the stages, approaches, and intensity levels of the interview process, as the polyphasic flowchart in Figure 9.1 shows. These categories will take on more meaning as we proceed, but for now, allow the flowchart to serve as a road map for the interview process. Throughout an investigation, you will study, research, gather, and examine factual information that will help answer your questions.

THE HISTORICAL PHASE

The *historical phase* of the interview process begins long before the investigator and the interviewee ever meet. It covers all the attitudes and beliefs that the participants bring to the interview. These influences were learned, directly or indirectly, from our parents or caregivers in childhood and were picked up from other sources throughout life. Some of us carry a great deal of "garbage" in our intellectual and emotional "baggage," including biases and prejudices that hamper our productivity and effectiveness. We discussed the effect of biases and prejudices on our interviews in earlier chapters.

Undoubtedly, our emotional baggage influences and shapes our behavior during the interview process. Don't overlook or underestimate the importance of the historical phase. The more self-awareness you bring to each interview, the more effective you will be in the personal preparation phase, which we discussed in earlier chapters and which we reexamine now.

THE PERSONAL PREPARATION PHASE

All adults have the opportunity to modify the biases and negative attitudes they learned while growing up. As investigators, we can take a close look at ourselves and change those things about us that have a negative impact on the process of communication. In our personal rebuilding, we can pilot our abilities to use the positive interview tactics suggested in this book. It is up to us to look into our emotional baggage and modify its contents if necessary.

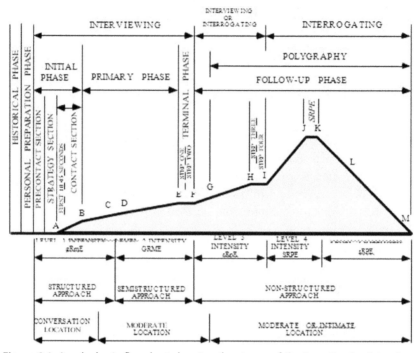

Figure 9.1 A polyphasic flowchart showing the stages of the investigative interview.

If we take the opportunity to discard much of the garbage, we will lead healthier lives. Through education, training, and experience, we can discard our biases and prejudices and become more proficient and effective investigators.

As we have seen, biases and prejudices lead to misguided observation, evaluation, and assessment, so professionals don't knowingly bring them into their inquiries. They acknowledge that how they treat people is greatly influenced by their past, but nevertheless, they remain in control of their own behavior.

All investigators are not equally talented in how they handle human interactions, but all interviewers can be applied scientists, discriminating among variables and using systematic, purposeful investigative methods. Investigators demonstrate their professional adaptability through their willingness to modify their behavior in a never-ending learning process. Their ethical behavior reveals itself as competence and leadership. Figure 9.2 provides another road map of the interview process, one that illustrates the thoughts and emotions behind the various stages.

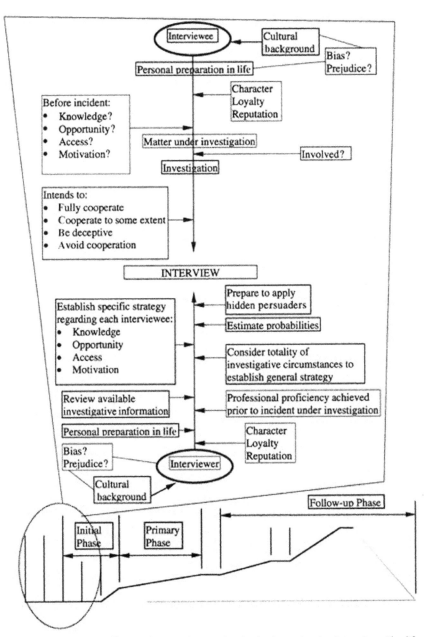

Figure 9.2 Elements affecting human interaction in the investigative interview. The life experiences of both the investigator and the interviewee come into play during the interview.

THE INITIAL PHASE

The fundamental purpose of the *initial phase* of the interview process is to consider detailed information regarding the incident under investigation, the people who might be involved, and the conditions under which the interviews will take place. The initial phase consists of three sections: pre-contact, strategic planning, and contact. The third section covers the first few critical minutes of each interview. We discuss each section in turn.

Precontact

During precontact (Figure 9.3), the interviewer becomes familiar with the available information about the matter under investigation and the various suspects and begins to formulate a flexible interview plan. This plan includes a clear picture of the objectives of the interview and a floating-point strategy.

The Floating-Point Strategy

Investigations are often based on probability and likelihood, and estimating the probability that a particular person committed the crime is the essence of the *floating-point strategy* (FPS). The FPS is a flexible problem-solving process that can be used in all inquiries. The investigator applies the FPS as soon as most of the elements of the investigative problem are known. The FPS allows the investigator to reevaluate and, if necessary, modify her operating hypothesis as new evidence is uncovered. Picture the problem-solving process as having numerous points at which you can reevaluate your progress and determine whether you are on the right track. Your strategy floats from point to point, never becoming fixed until you are reasonably sure of your assessment of the evidence.

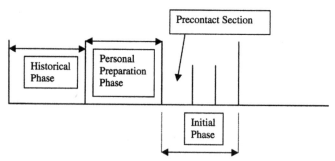

Figure 9.3 The precontact section of the initial phase. This is the time when the investigator gathers information about both the matter under investigation and the suspects.

The Preliminary Inquiry

During the precontact section, the investigator collects evidence and reviews information collected from victims and witnesses. The success of an investigation is often based on how thoroughly the investigator gathers this preliminary data. Specific details about the incident form the foundation to which the investigator will refer throughout the investigation. Clues about motivation may be found in the lifestyle, habits, hobbies, stressors, and needs of the suspects. Be careful conducting the preliminary inquiry! The person who provides the preliminary information in an investigation may have a hidden agenda—a plan to deceive you and mislead you by providing false information. Look for the telltale signs of deception: inconsistencies, illogical details, information clouded by fear or anger. Watch for calculated attempts to obscure the facts.

Strategic Planning

Experienced investigators make interviewing look easier than it is. The novice interviewer may watch the casual performance of the experienced interviewer and incorrectly assume that the relaxed prevailing emotional tone or attitude of the experienced interviewer indicates that she has done no important or noticeable research or planning. In fact, *strategic planning*, the second section of the initial phase, is an important part of the interview process (Figure 9.4). During this section, the investigator evaluates potential interviewees, prepares an interview strategy based on what she has learned, and prepares psychologically for the interview.

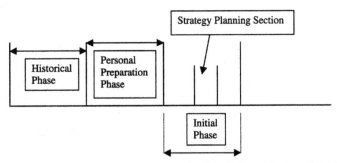

Figure 9.4 The strategic planning section of the initial phase. During this phase, the investigator considers all aspects of the planned interviews, including where they will be held and in what order the suspects will be interviewed.

Evaluating Potential Interviewees

Before conducting any interviews, the investigator evaluates each potential interviewee based on information provided by people close to the investigation. The investigator then calculates the chances of gaining truthful testimonial evidence from each person.

This calculation is a subjective estimate, nothing more than thoughts about whether someone will be easy or hard to interview. The investigator also considers how well he will get along with each interviewee and how cooperative that person will be. As you prepare for an investigation, you will probably need to evaluate potential interviewees sight unseen, based on the preliminary information you are given.

Creating an Interview Strategy

The goal of an investigative interview is to gain as much truthful information as possible. You want interviewees to tell you everything they know about the matter under investigation. Interviewees have the power of information—information you need to conclude the investigation successfully. As discussed earlier, many factors determine whether interviewees decide to relinquish or hold onto this information. It is important, therefore, to plan an appropriate strategy for each interview. It is better to be overprepared than underprepared, especially when you're dealing with people who might try to deceive you.[1]

Interviewees are selected on the basis of their knowledge, opportunity, access, and motivation related to the matter under investigation. Planning for an interview might include conducting a background check of the interviewee. Having advance information about the interviewee allows the investigator to anticipate whether the person will cooperate and helps the investigator prepare an appropriate strategy for the interview. Awareness of interviewees' attitudes and feelings can help you mold yourself to meet their personalities and counter potential reluctance. Preparing for reluctance is vital, though you should always expect compliance. In most instances, though, the investigator has little or no specific knowledge about potential interviewees before beginning an investigation.

Before conducting an interview, plan how you will behave during the encounter. How will you speak, and how will you act? How will you show energy, strength, and concentration? To what extent will you review

[1] Quinn and Zunin, 1972.

details with the interviewee? Will your review of details help the interviewee remember additional information? How will you encourage the interviewee to be truthful? If your encouragement is inspired with courage, spirit, and confidence, you will probably gain pertinent and helpful information.

Preparing Psychologically for the Interview

Plan to enter each interview with an open mind. This means not only keeping your mind open to the guilt or innocence of each suspect but being accepting and nonjudgmental, even when you are interacting with those you have designated prime suspects. In addition, be determined to put misinformation aside and think for yourself. Don't accept any piece of information until you have evaluated it in light of the other evidence.

Use positive expectations in all efforts to gather information. In other words, treat interviewees as though they want to comply. In everything you do and say, act as though you know the interviewee truly wants to cooperate with the investigation. Most interviewees do, in fact, respond positively to this expectation.

Positive behavior is necessary if you are to achieve proficiency as an interviewer. Excellent interviewers modify their behavior to inspire and convince interviewees to provide truthful information, and with sufficient practice and dedication, many develop into capable interrogators. By applying honed interviewing skills and focusing your energies on improvement, you will become competent at solving complicated investigative problems. It's not force but finesse that counts in human interaction.

Contact

A and B of the polyphasic flowchart (refer back to Figure 9.1) define the first four minutes of the actual interview. Thus span of time is the *contact section* of the initial phase (Figure 9.5). Your main purpose during these first four minutes is to establish a rapport with the interviewee. You will develop skills such as imagination, creativity, flexibility, and other skills that will help uncover information through ways other than direct question-and-answer statements. You will continue to use these tactics throughout the interview, even into the follow-up phase, when inconsistencies are resolved, confrontation takes place, and admissions and confessions are sought and obtained.

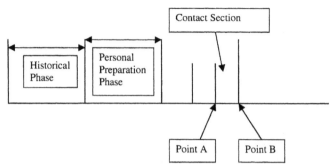

Figure 9.5 The contact section of the initial phase (the first four minutes of each interview). The investigator and the interviewee have their first verbal and nonverbal exchanges during this time.

UNCOVERING THE TRUTH

Over time you will learn a variety of ways to gather information during an interview. Building rapport with the interviewee, maintaining a positive attitude, and active listening all help the interviewer display favorable characteristics. They show the interviewee that the interviewer can be trusted. If they are applied sensitively and skillfully, they will have significant and positive effects on the outcome of your interviews.

In most interviews, the investigator has at least one agenda, whether obvious or hidden. The hidden one is an unannounced reason for conducting the interview. For example, one hidden agenda when you're interviewing a victim is to determine whether a crime actually took place. The rapport you build and your attitude will help conceal the interviewer's true agenda and will help the investigator outsmart the interviewee.

Consider the human needs of interview participants:

- Build and maintain rapport.
- Maintain a positive attitude.
- Apply flexible methods.
- Cover suspiciousness.
- Use creative imagination.
- Exhibit human warmth, sensitivity, empathy, respect, and genuineness.
- Be nonjudgmental.
- Listen actively.
- Be attentive.
- Be patient.

- Be positive: Use positive silence, positive eye contact, positive personal space, positive body motions (kinesics) and body language, and positive touch when appropriate.
- Cover personal values.
- Maintain a positive, neutral stance.
- Use positive power and positive control.
- Control personal anger; avoid antagonizing or harassing interviewees.
- Don't use coercive behavior.
- Use observation, evaluation, and assessment.
- Avoid the third degree (mental or physical torture used in an effort to gain a confession).
- Use closed questions and open questions when appropriate.
- Keep questions simple; avoid ambiguously worded questions.
- Dare to ask tough questions.
- Mentally assume an affirmative answer.
- Use leading questions appropriately and ask self-appraisal questions.
- Handle trial balloons calmly.
- Assume that more information is available.

First Impressions

You make your first impression during the initial 10 to 45 seconds of an interview. This is your opportunity to show that you are fair, nonjudgmental, friendly, calm, cool, collected, human, and compassionate. First impressions are important in helping to cement a close, but building a relationship is instrumental in encouraging the interviewee's cooperation. In those first seconds of human interaction, you convey your intentions through nonverbal messages. You express human warmth through your tone of voice and your gestures and mannerisms. These things significantly affect the outcome of an interview.

Although face-to-face interviews are preferred, telephone interviews are sometimes necessary. In a telephone interview, you can express your positive qualities through your tone of voice, timing, and silences.

On occasion, an interviewee will confess or make some significant admission within the first few minutes of the interview without being specifically encouraged to do so. Be ready for this possibility.

The Interviewee's Evaluation Process

Observation, evaluation, assessment, and intuition are vital elements of investigative problem solving. The interviewee's *evaluation process* usually begins with the first verbal and nonverbal exchanges in an encounter, and they continue until the end. You can expect the interviewee to start an evaluation process with his or her first glimpse of you. How do you look? Do you appear to be a professional? How do you sound—overbearing? Are you portraying yourself as warm and caring? Consciously or subconsciously, even the slowest, least educated interviewees evaluate you to decide whether it is safe to reveal information or whether they will be abused in the process. The interviewee's evaluation process takes place whether you want it to or not. Remember that your tone of voice, choice of words, and body language express particular attitudes. This is the time to signal that you want the interview to be a friendly interaction.

Subsequent interviewees will evaluate the interview process in part based on how you treated preceding interviewees. The message about you and your methods will be conveyed to everyone—that you are okay or not, fair or not, biased or not. There is no question that you will be judged.

There is some strategic advantage if the interviewee is not under arrest when interviewed; faced with less of a threat, the interviewee experiences less distress and is more likely to cooperate. Although the interviewee may still be uncomfortable, your professional demeanor and friendly ways will make you seem worthy of receiving important information. This is common in the private investigation world. Throughout my 32 years in the business, it has been very easy to get interviewees to talk with me. Each interview is different, and you, the investigator or internal security person, will use different elements. Your style, demonstrated level of respect, and experience will determine your success. If you seem disarming and are experienced at using your developed skills, you can get anyone to talk with you.

Elements of Contact
Introduction and Greeting
A formal introduction will help establish you as someone in whom it is safe to confide. When possible, it is useful to separate yourself from any prior investigations of the crime you are asked to solve. For example, I speak softly, not in a weak fashion but in a modulated tone that I hope will convey my confidence and human warmth. I might say, "Hello, I'm Ms. Black. Would you follow me, please?" as I meet the interviewee in a waiting room before we walk to my office down the hall. Then, when we reach my office, I may say, "Please, have a seat here," as I motion to a particular chair.

During the first few minutes, the tone of the interview is determined, and it may last for minutes, hours, or days. If an interviewee offers to shake hands when we meet, then I do, but I don't routinely offer a handshake to each interviewee. I usually try to maintain a professional aloofness to signal the serious nature of the inquiry. I try to appear reserved, not stuffy. Although having been trained by Wicklander in which one method is to make small talk, I really have never spent much time, if any, on small talk. Every interviewer and investigator has different methods and styles, but I usually felt that if I was conducting an interview for an internal investigation, I was doing it only after I had enough evidence. My approach is to find a way for the interviewee/suspect to tell me what they have done. One of my methods would be to tell the interviewee that I was working with the company's audit department and we were looking into the loss of assets and hoping they would be able to assist us in resolving this issue. Of course, I always had videotapes, statements from witnesses, or other evidence I made the interviewee aware of. At no time did I mention law enforcement, prosecution, or arrest. That gave the interviewee the impression that they were assisting in explaining the losses without thinking about possible consequences associated with a crime. It was often the fact that I used phrases like *shortages, justification, balancing,* and *auditing* rather than *stealing, theft, prosecution,* or *police.*

Of course, that is the intent and ultimate mission, but the main objective during the interview is to get the evidence, confession, and statement. Always assume that you are going to get this confession and statement because it will help you be prepared with the necessary company documents and all the evidence when the police arrive. Once the confession is made, I always had a minute to leave the room, leaving another witness with the suspect, so that I could make the call to local law enforcement. It was often quite a surprise when the police would arrive, because the suspect didn't make the connection between helping balance the shortages and being convicted of a crime.

Each interview is unique, which is why practice and experience are what will develop your skills as an investigative interviewer.

Back in the 1980s, interviews were more of the interrogation type, and we didn't have to concern ourselves with how long we kept interviewees or how we acquired their statements. In fact, many interviewees' statements were written by me or other investigators, with the interviewees or suspects signing them. Since then the investigation field has become more professional, with a higher level of training and ethics. Today we should avoid all forms of intimidation and abusiveness that might in any way spark resentment or defensiveness. My goal is to have victims, witnesses, and suspects alike feel that they can talk to me.

Greeting interviewees cordially helps them feel at ease. Despite your innocent manner, try your best to encourage them to provide the information you need. Help interviewees relax enough that they do not feel threatened, but bear in mind that eliminating all tension is neither possible nor to your advantage. Some degree of tension in an interview often helps the interviewee think actively so that the interview, including the response, is productive.

Seating

For the interview, choose a location that provides both privacy and comfort. Determine the seating arrangements in advance. The main point to remember is that *you* are in control. Use this control to arrange the chairs so that you are sitting across from the interviewee. You will want to have the interviewee sitting where he can't escape the room easily but you can. You don't want the interviewee being distracted, so keep the room uncluttered. As the interview progresses, I usually move my chair to within about four feet of the interviewee. I try to use chairs of similar design and comfort. Obviously, chairs and their location are a ridiculous consideration at an accident scene, but the important point is to avoid moving too fast into the interviewee's personal space. Controlling the interview room also means that you want to be sitting in a place that will avoid direct sunlight with your back to the wall, in a room that is temperature controlled and not overheating. You want to be sure to take water with you.

Announcing Your Objective

Announce the objective of the interview in answer to the interviewee's usually unasked question about why she is being interviewed. Tell the interviewee that you want to determine how the incident that you're investigating happened and that you want to prevent similar events from occurring in the future. For example, you might say, "The purpose of our talk today is to discuss some electronic kitchen appliances that seem to be missing from the warehouse. I'm looking for information that will help me determine how these appliances were removed so that I can make clear recommendations to prevent another disappearance in the future. I'm interviewing several people, and I need your assistance to get a better view of the circumstances. First, let me get a little background data about you to get to know you a little better." By orienting interviewees to the objective of your interview, you encourage them to be less secretive and defensive. When they realize the seriousness of your inquiry, interviewees may comply more completely. As I mentioned, never announce your objective as identifying and prosecuting the guilty party. Although interviewees often want to know how their interview is relevant and significant to your inquiry, it is not helpful to explain your overall objectives. Too much explanation may cause them to become apprehensive about how their help might harm fellow human beings, reducing their willingness to cooperate. Alternatively, they might not accept your explanation and might provide only limited information that might not be truthful or helpful. Hence, too much explanation unnecessarily gives interviewees directive powers—the power to lead an interview down a particular path.

When beginning an interview, adopt an open manner that invites the interviewee to share any thoughts, observations, opinions, or facts that have any bearing on the crime. This invitation should be implied, not actually spoken, and you should show appreciation for the cooperation when it comes. If there is a time to open the door to the truth, it is at this point of the discussion—in the first four minutes, when the interviewee is determining whether it is okay to talk to you. In those first minutes, the interviewee senses whether you are neutral or biased, whether you are trying to gather facts or are taking unfair advantage of people.

Setting the Tone

After you have announced the objective and during those critical first few minutes of the interaction, ask the interviewee questions that will be easy to answer: the spelling of his or her name, date of birth, number of years of employment, current position, years of education, marital status. These questions give the interviewee the opportunity to vent some emotional energy and to feel more comfortable. At this stage of the investigation, you may note evasiveness and lack of cooperation. From the beginning, use positive tactics that encourage cooperation, such as active listening, empathy, respect, and believability.

Forensic interviews are not intense interactions in which verbal combat takes place. Try for a soft harmony to promote comfort and thought. Use a toned-down style to avoid any suggestion of intense confrontation. In discussing the circumstances of an incident, I recommend that you use the word *if* to soften the questioning. Using *if* tends to prevent any implied accusation in your voice. Too often investigators interrogate every interviewee in a prosecutorial manner in hopes of quickly unmasking the guilty party. I see no justification for treating every interviewee as though he were guilty. I avoid using quick questions and burning stares. At the outset of each interview, my choice of words and phrases is intended to exhibit my positive attitude and expectations. Setting a positive tone with each interviewee pays off. Doing so communicates a professional self-image.

Contact at the Crime Scene

At a crime scene, the victim's fear is so immediate and powerful that it cannot be dissipated by the victim's exercise of self-control alone. Your patience and assistance will be required. A hurried approach will only cause confusion and heighten the victim's distress. Calm the victim by saying something like, "You're safe now." Showing proper regard for the victim's feelings builds empathy, which facilitates questioning and promotes accurate recollections. Fear of reprisal and intimidation may prevent witnesses as well as victims from cooperating; to prevent intimidation, move witnesses away from suspects before identifying and interviewing them. Ask witnesses to recall everything observed during the incident; be sure that you don't contaminate the information they provide. For example, as a witness presents recall, avoid editorializing by interpreting as the recall progresses; otherwise you may find that the recall tends to follow your expectation or interpretation. Therefore, keep your evaluation to yourself so as not to influence the recall.

Because of the urgency of some criminal investigations, it is not always possible to prepare fully for an interview. In such a situation, gather basic information immediately; later, in a recontact interview, obtain additional facts under more favorable conditions. Remember, though, that the greater the time lapse between the incident and the interview, the less likely it is that witnesses will be able to accurately report what they observed. In addition, they may be reluctant to cooperate fully once the excitement of the situation has subsided. Contamination is another concern. People tend to seek group consensus, and they will often adopt the group opinion as their own, regardless of whether they believe it to be correct. If not separated quickly and interviewed, witnesses may compare stories and adopt parts of the accounts of others at the crime scene. Make a special point of interviewing alibi witnesses promptly to reduce the possibility that suspect and witness will take the opportunity to corroborate their stories and cover up the suspect's participation in the crime.

THE PRIMARY PHASE

The *primary phase* follows the contact section of the initial phase of the interview. During the primary phase, the interviewer strengthens the rapport

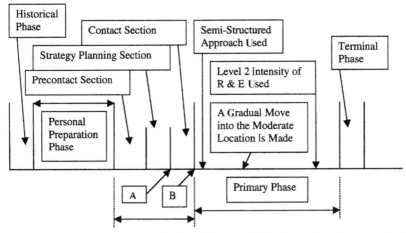

Figure 9.6 The primary phase. During this part of the interview, the investigator observes, evaluates, and assesses the interviewee's verbal and nonverbal behavior.

begun in the contact section, gathers more information through active listening, and watches for signs of deception. By this point, you have established that you are open to discussion, and when you are seen as a warm person, you are more likely to gain the information you are seeking.

At the beginning of the primary phase (Figure 9.6), the interviewer gradually moves his or her chair closer to the interviewee (the moderate location discussed in Chapter 10). Between points B and C of the interview process (Figure 9.7), the investigator reviews the case information with the interviewee as a prelude to asking additional questions. All the while, he or she tries to maintain a positive tone and build rapport.

Exactly how you will proceed—which questions you will ask and how you will formulate them—depends as much on the quality of the interaction you have been able to establish as on the facts you need to gather. The investigator's adaptability is vital. Being able to think on your feet is important to seeking out the truth. (See Chapter 11 for more on question formulation.) The investigator moves from a structured to a semistructured approach between points C and D on the polyphasic flowchart (refer back to Figure 9.1). Encourage interviewees to think carefully and to try to remember details. Allow them the time they need to think. Don't interrogate yet! That will come later.

"Bones"

Around points C and D on the flowchart, I begin to use what I call *bones*— nonaccusatory questions that reveal the elements of the complete incident.

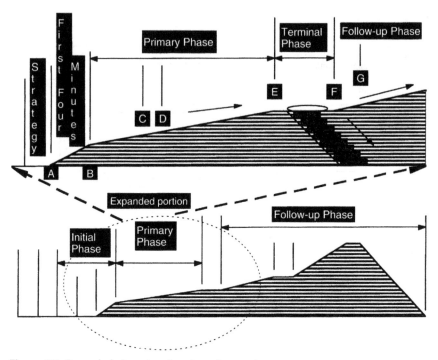

Figure 9.7 Expanded view showing the primary phase.

These semistructured questions work together much as the bones of the body make up a whole skeleton. In the same way that muscle and tissue surround our bones, all the details of the incident and the interviewee's involvement surround the central facts of the incident. The semistructured questions you use in this phase of the interview are designed to reveal, through an interviewee's pattern of responses, whether she is lying or telling the truth.

Move with compassion and continue to use the hidden persuaders throughout the primary phase. Without being obvious, try to imply that you are seeking the interviewee's permission to ask the questions as you proceed. Avoid hasty conclusions and accusations. Don't abruptly stop interviewing and begin trying to gain an admission or confession. Remember that culpable individuals hesitate to reveal a truth that brings shame, embarrassment, and possible punishment. As a lead-in to using the bones, you might say, "As I mentioned before, I'm trying to determine how the loss occurred. So, let me ask you a few questions." Then proceed with the following series of questions, remembering to remain flexible and keeping in mind the value of the floating-point strategy.

The Narration Question

At some logical point during the primary phase, ask the interviewee to tell you what happened—what he knows of the incident under investigation. Truthful interviewees tend to provide smooth- flowing narratives that have been clearly thought out. They may offer suggestions to help you solve the matter. Untruthful interviewees will weigh everything they say, causing awkward pauses in their narration. Once the narrative is complete, review and summarize the details to ensure that the report is complete. Allow the interviewee unrestricted recall, and then ask specific questions to uncover details. All the while take notes to show that you are attentive.

The "You" Question

Address the interviewee by name, and begin this question by saying, "It's important to get this matter cleared up." Briefly review the reported incident and explain that you are asking these questions in an effort to determine what happened. The "you" question might take several forms. Here are a few examples:

- "If you're the one who did it, it's important to get it cleared up. How do you stand on this? Did you steal the traveler's checks?"
- "The report claims that you spoke with Rita just before the fire broke out. If you did, it's important to get this straightened out and clear things up. Jim, let me ask, did you have any contact with Rita just before the fire broke out?"

An interviewee who has a high level of shame and remorse and cannot stand the stress of the investigation may provide a full confession at this point. This is a rare occurrence, however. Do not ask the "you" question accusingly, and do nothing to suggest that the interviewee is responsible for the incident or is lying. Instead, adopt a positive tone of open curiosity. "If the interviewee is hiding something, your genuine curiosity will provoke unease and evasion exhibited by such outward signs as squirming and preening. Such signs of evasion and possible deception may take place in about a hundredth of a second. You should be attentive and notice these signals without being obvious.

The "Who" Question

You might begin the "who" question with a preamble, such as, "Knowing for sure who did set the fire in the warehouse is one thing, but having suspicions is something else. Do you know for sure who set the fire?" The interviewee will probably answer negatively, which leads easily into the next question.

The "Suspicion" Question

Then you might say, "Okay, you don't know for sure who did it. But let me ask: Do you have any suspicions of who might have set the fire?" Quickly add the caveat, "Keep in mind that I'm not asking you to be malicious, to arbitrarily point a finger at anyone or anything like that, because that wouldn't be fair. I'm just wondering if anyone has done anything or said anything to cause you to think they might have set the fire. Can you think of anyone who might have been involved?" Typical responses from non-culpable interviewees include these: "I can't imagine who did it or why"; "I can't believe it even happened here"; "If one of my coworkers did it, he would have to be a Jekyll-and-Hyde personality."

The "Trust" Question

This question usually takes the form, "Who comes to mind that you trust? Who do you think could not possibly have stolen the computer equipment?" or "Of all the people who had the opportunity, who do you think would *not* have taken the money?"

The "Verification" Question

"After considering the situation, do you think the money was really stolen, or do you think the theft report is false?" Culpable interviewees may say they don't think the loss was caused by theft: "It must have been a mistake or misplaced in some way." The blameless tend to acknowledge the report as correct, saying the theft was real.

The "Approach" Question

"Life presents many temptations for all of us. Let me ask you this: Have any of the truckers ever asked you to divert a cargo?" The blameless interviewee acknowledges that there was some discussion but that he never took it seriously enough to mention. The culpable ones latch onto such discussions as an opportunity to cast blame on others and report that discussions took place.

The "Thoughts" Question

"There are so many demands and pressures on people in their daily lives that they occasionally fantasize about doing things. Now, as far as you're concerned, do you recall ever thinking of having sex with Mary Sue, even though you never actually did?" To report a fantasy of having sex with Mary Sue tells me that the culpable interviewee considers the thinking meaningful, memorable enough to recall. "Well, there have been times when she rubs herself against me and I think she really wants me to touch her sexually." The innocent do not consider such fleeting moments significant and deny involvement.

The "Instruction" Question

This question is useful when you're investigating charges of child sexual abuse. "Many people teach their kids about sex as they're growing up. After all, it's the responsibility of the parent to teach their children about things like health. You certainly don't want anyone taking advantage of them. What comes to mind about telling your kids things about sex?"

The "Willingness" Question

"If the investigation shows that you actually did leave the store with groceries you didn't pay for, would you be willing to explain it and get this matter straightened out? Would you be willing to pay for those missing things?"

The "Consequences" Questions

The next few questions ask the interviewee about the consequences of certain actions. For example, you might ask, "Let's assume that we find out the report was not true. What should happen to Jane for her false accusation?" Then give time for the response and do not rush to ask the second question: "If we find out who took Jane's purse, what should happen to that person?" The culpable will want to give the thief a break, whereas the nonculpable will want to see the culpable caught.

If the interviewee does not suggest jail for the guilty party, ask, "How about jail for that person?" Innocent interviewees usually respond, "I should think so! That pervert!" or something to that effect. They answer smoothly, giving their judgment without hesitation. The deceptive, on the other hand, tend to be lenient toward the guilty party or evasive in their responses. They might say, for example, "Well, jail seems a little harsh," or "It really depends on the circumstances. Maybe the person was under a lot of stress." Then later, stress could be the basis of an interrogative approach.

The "Kind to Do It" Question

Your next question might be, "What kind of person do you think would do something like this?" Nonculpable people quickly provide an appropriate response, such as, "Some sick person!" or "Someone who doesn't care about making us go through this." The deceptive will tend to rationalize or evade the question, responding, "Someone who is under a lot of pressure!" or "I'm not that kind of person! I'm not a pervert!"

The "Why It Happened" Question

Then you might ask, "Why do you think a person would do this sort of thing?" You might expect the nonculpable to respond quickly and clearly, "I have no idea," whereas the culpable might respond, "No reason!" or "There's a divorce case!" or "The people here aren't paid enough!" The culpable often try to give the thief an excuse or rationalization.

The "They Say You Did It" Question

When you ask, "Is there any reason for anyone to say you broke into the storeroom?" innocent interviewees might respond, "No, I don't think so. I didn't do it." They will appear to consider whether they could have given anyone a reason to suspect them. Rather than squirm and look guilty, they may furrow their brow, squint, or look contemplative. This body language is fleeting and difficult to fake convincingly.

The "They Say They Saw You" Question

Follow up the preceding question with, "Is there any reason that anyone might say they saw you breaking into the storeroom?" The innocent might say, "No, because I didn't do it!" They will respond quickly and without contemplation because they don't need deep thought to know what they did. The culpable party might say, "Well, let me see. . . . Uh, no, I don't think so."

The "What Would You Say" Question

This question asks the interviewee to think about the person responsible for the incident. Ask something like this: "Let's assume that the ring was actually stolen. If the guilty person were here standing before you, what would you say to him or her?" Interviewees with nothing to hide often respond, "What you did was wrong!" or "That was a stupid thing to do!" The response will come quickly and smoothly, often as an angry blast of indignation and condemnation. Deceptive interviewees will often be hard-pressed to find words of condemnation.

The "Expanding Inquiry" Question

"Do you mind having the investigation extend beyond your family to your neighbors and coworkers?" The culpable may hesitate to have an inquiry go out of the immediate work area. If it is brought to the attention of friends and neighbors, someone may comment on what seemed like suspicious behavior, such as a recent vacation or a large purchase. The nonculpable ones don't mind the extended inquiry because they generally don't have anything to hide.

THE TERMINAL PHASE

Between points E and F of the polyphasic flowchart (refer back to Figure 9.1) lies the terminal phase, a turning point in the interview. During this phase, the investigator draws a conclusion about the interviewee's veracity. The interviewer synthesizes all of the interviewee's verbal and nonverbal responses into a significant pattern indicating one of the following:

- Truthfulness
- Probable truthfulness
- Possible truthfulness
- Possible deception
- Probable deception
- Deception

The first step in the terminal phase is to determine whether the interviewee has answered your questions fully and truthfully. The second step involves planning what to do next.

Step 1

By the beginning of the terminal phase, you will have had the opportunity to observe, evaluate, and assess the interviewee, noting how the pattern of her responses compares to the totality of the evidence. You will have had enough time to become confident in your conclusion. Generally, one interview will offer sufficient indicators to guide your conclusions, but not always. There are certainly no absolutes in such assessments, but I'm convinced that nonverbal signals are meaningful indicators of deception. I think it's fair to say, based on my experience, that certain behavior signals characterize deceptive individuals, whereas other behavior signals characterize the truthful. When interviewees are inconsistent or deceptive, it is as though they are trying to force a blue puzzle piece into a space intended for a brown piece. Differences become evident when the investigator considers the totality of the circumstances.

Even cooperative interviewees might show some indications of holding back information. Victims may hide some of the details of an incident because they are embarrassed over their victimization. Witnesses may appear to be holding back information because they feel self-conscious about not having done more to aid the victim or stop the thief. On the other hand, inconsistencies in a victim's or witness's story may indicate that she fabricated the crime. Perhaps the interviewee actually stole the money herself or arranged for a buddy to steal it in a mock holdup. A witness who was a co-conspirator in the crime has good reason to feel uneasy over being questioned about the details of the incident. And of course, the perpetrator will try to hold back information. Criminals with little practice tend to stumble over routine investigative questions, showing telltale signs of involvement.

For a variety of reasons, investigators sometimes enter the terminal phase of an interview without having reached a conclusion about the interviewee's truthfulness. If this occurs, you might try one of the following:

- Comment that it looks as though the interviewee has more information to provide.
- Tell the interviewee that a second interview will be set up in the near future to review a few things.
- Give the impression that you suspect that the interviewee is hiding or holding back important information.

Step 2

By the end of the terminal phase, after using both the structured and semi-structured approaches, evaluate whether there is a need for further interviewing using the unstructured approach or whether it would be appropriate to seek an admission or a confession through interrogation.

If this is to be the end of the interview, leave your business card and ask the interviewee to contact you if he or she remembers anything new. If there are inconsistencies that you want to clarify, you might decide to continue the interview or to schedule another. To verify information that the interviewee has supplied, you might try to schedule a detection-of-deception examination. No matter what course you choose, maintain rapport. This is not a time to put on the nasty-guy hat.

THE FOLLOW-UP PHASE

The last phase of the interview process is the *follow-up phase*, which occurs between points F and M on the polyphasic flowchart (refer back to Figure 9.1). During this final phase of the interview process, inconsistencies are resolved, confrontation may take place, and confessions may be obtained. At this point, you have considerable flexibility in applying the floating-point strategy. Maintain rapport, continue to listen actively, and avoid radical direction (changes of a sweeping or extreme nature) or any use of abuse, coercion, harassment, or intimidation.

Between flowchart points F and G, you might decide to review the interviewee's responses, point out inconsistencies, and hint at the interviewee's deception. Seek the truth using increased review and encouragement at this turning point. Proceed cautiously. A premature announcement of your suspicions may only encourage the interviewee to do a better job of covering the truth.

Step 3

Depending on the circumstances of the investigation, you may decide to pursue one of the following courses:
- Arrange for the interviewee to take a detection-of-deception examination.
- Schedule a new interview with the interviewee, allowing yourself time to prepare for a second interview and possible interrogation.
- Begin an attempt to gain an admission or confession from the subject.

Once interviewees claim that the information they are providing is truthful, you can ask whether they would be willing to undergo a detection-of-deception (polygraph) examination. This suggestion might be made at several places during the process: between points G and H, between points H and I, or about point L on the flowchart. The timing depends on the situation and on how the suggestion fits into the overall process. Some people will not agree to undergo a polygraph examination, no matter how helpful you tell them it will be. Others will be reluctant but will eventually submit to it.

There are two important things to consider before requesting that an interviewee undergo a polygraph examination. First, it is important to be convinced that the polygraph is a practical, functional, and trustworthy investigative tool. Second, you should ensure that the forensic psychophysiologist chosen to administer the examination will provide high-quality, professional service. Although polygraph examinations are not 100 percent accurate, they have proved to be highly reliable.

Step 4

After attempting to resolve inconsistencies in the interviewee's story between points F and H, you may decide to take further action. If you are convinced that the interviewee is involved, directly or indirectly, in the matter under investigation, you will reveal this between points H and I. If you are ready to point out inconsistencies in the interviewee's story, the next thing to do is to announce your conclusion to the interviewee. To begin the interrogation, you might confront the subject by saying, for example:

- "It looks as if you haven't told me the whole truth."
- "It seems to me that you are holding something back."
- "I'm uneasy about what you've told me here today. I believe you've got more to tell me."
- "I think you're the one who did it, and it's important for us to talk about this to get it cleared up."

Use care when making such statements. You don't want to frighten the subject. For an investigator to express such a conclusion takes some daring and skill. Although there is no need to harshly accuse or intimidate the interviewee, this is the time for specific review and persistent encouragement to clear up inconsistencies or to gain an admission or a confession. It is at this point that the interview gradually flows into an interrogation. The interviewer-turned-interrogator now clearly and specifically announces that the subject seems to be intentionally withholding information and is probably a key player in the matter under investigation. While you announce your suspicions, you should continue to help the subject save face and rationalize his involvement. This is no time to degrade or humiliate the subject. Coercion has no place here—or indeed anywhere in this process.

Up to this time, you have modified your efforts to deal with embarrassed victims and reluctant witnesses, but now is the time to forge ahead into an interrogation to seek an admission or a confession. Don't be destructive in your efforts. Don't label the interviewee when addressing him. In other words, don't say, "I know you're the molester." Not only are such comments hostile, but they are self-defeating.

Be certain, and be confident! This is no longer the time for using the word *if*. Instead, display confidence in the subject's involvement. Interrogation is not for all investigators. It is a matter of temperament, confidence, and skill. Some investigators are more capable than others of handling this concentrated search for the truth.

Your efforts may yield only an incomplete admission of guilt. If you doubt that the subject told the complete story of what happened, remember that even a partial confession can be helpful in concluding the investigation. That is not to say that you should be satisfied with a half-done job. Accept whatever confession or admission is offered, and have it witnessed and put into written form. Then commit yourself to starting over with renewed effort to seek more details of the subject's culpability.

REVIEW QUESTIONS

1. How and when do we learn bias and prejudice?
2. How can we change our attitudes as we mature?
3. Name the three sections of the initial phase, and describe the interviewer's task in each.
4. What is the floating-point strategy, and how can you use it during an investigation?
5. Where can you find hints of motivation?
6. How can you evaluate potential interviewees, and why should you do this?
7. What should you consider in planning an interview strategy?
8. What does it mean to have an open mind as an interviewer?
9. What is the main purpose of the first four minutes of an interview?
10. What are hidden persuaders, and how can you use them in an interview?
11. Which of the hidden persuaders do you think are most effective?
12. How can you make a positive impression in the first few seconds of an interview?
13. How does the interviewee evaluate the investigator? What is she trying to determine?
14. What is the strategic advantage in interviewing someone who is not under arrest?
15. What are the elements of the contact section?
16. What should you tell the interviewee about the objective of the interview?
17. How can you put the interviewee at ease to promote cooperation?

18. What tactics can you use when you're interviewing victims and witnesses at a crime scene?
19. What is the interviewer's task in the primary phase?
20. What are "bones," and what do they help the interviewer determine?
21. Why is it useful to have the interviewee provide a narrative of what happened?
22. What is the interviewer's task in the terminal phase?
23. What occurs during the follow-up phase?
24. What might you say to the subject as you flow from interviewing into interrogating?

CHAPTER 10

Setting, Location, Intensity, and Approach in the Interview

To ensure the success of an interview, investigators must consider many factors, including where the interview will take place, how the participants will be positioned within the interview room, how intensely the interviewer will press for information, and what approach the interviewer will use in questioning the interviewee. All these elements require careful planning because they have a significant impact on the outcome of every interview. This chapter suggests ways in which environmental setting, participant location, intensity, and approach can be incorporated into the interview process.

ENVIRONMENTAL SETTING

As a private investigator, my interviews are usually dictated by where I can find the interviewee. Planning when and where to find the interviewee is my priority, but after that, privacy is an important element of successful interviews. In a perfect world, you would have a comfortable, private room, but this is not always possible. Your goal is to obtain information through the interview. You will want to conduct your interview in a private space, quiet and free from disturbances. There is little to gain by transporting interviewees to some distant site that you think is ideal. Doing so might cause unnecessary disruption. Focus on opportunity, space, and availability and, of course, the questions.

I have sat in my car for hours waiting for my interviewee to be alone.

LOCATION OF PARTICIPANTS

Personal Space

There is an invisible boundary, known as *personal space*, around each of us. We become uncomfortable when strangers intrude in our personal space. Most Americans reserve about a foot and a half of space around them for intimate conversation. They allow casual interactions in the space between about a foot and a half to about four feet. Impersonal transactions take place beyond about four feet. Personal space varies depending on culture, social status, personal history, and upbringing. Sometimes people of high status assume and are granted more personal space than people of lower status.

Proxemics is the study of the spatial distances that people maintain between themselves and others. Knowledge of proxemics can help you become a better interviewer. Recognize that there may be an invisible boundary that surrounds your interviewee. Whether standing or sitting during an interview, be sensitive to the interviewee's level of comfort and use it to determine how the interviewee defines his or her personal space. Enter this space with care to avoid alarming the interviewee. Moving too quickly into the interviewee's personal space may cause undue stress, which might restrict the flow of communication.

Conversation, Moderate, and Intimate Locations

I believe that it is helpful to identify three distinct distances between interview participants. In order of decreasing physical distance, I call these the *conversation*, *moderate*, and *intimate locations*. When I say *location*, I mean to include both distance and position. Most interviews take place in the conversation or moderate location.

As you begin the interview, position yourself in the conversation location, about six feet away from the interviewee, and then gradually move closer into the moderate location, where you can conduct most of the interview. Not only does moving closer convey your warmth, but also it will help both you and the interviewee focus more fully on the discussion. The display of positive motives generally sparks productive results. The intimate locations are used when the interviewee needs comforting, when using intensity level 4 (reviewed later in the chapter), or during other portions of the follow-up phase. Of course, space limitations may prevent you from beginning the interview in the conversation location or moving closer to the interviewee than the moderate location.

The Conversation Location

In the *conversation location*, the interview participants are situated about six feet apart, as shown in Figures 10.1 and 10.2. This is a "safe" distance for the interviewee, just beyond easy physical reach. In this location, participants have enough room to lean forward without touching and can move their legs comfortably. The conversation location permits the investigator to observe the interviewee for nonverbal communication at critical moments. The conversation location is used between points A and C of the polyphasic flowchart shown in Chapter 9 (refer back to Figure 9.1).

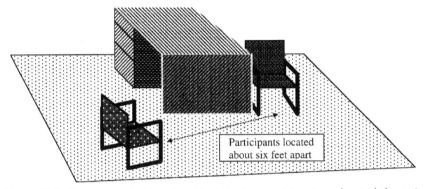

Figure 10.1 The conversation location. The interview participants are located about six feet apart.

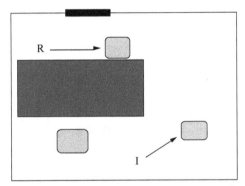

Figure 10.2 Overhead view of a typical interview room, 10 by 12 feet, showing participants in the conversation location. *I* = interviewer; *R* = respondent.

At the beginning of the interview, position your chair to the left or right of the interviewee's chair at an angle of about 45 degrees. Avoid facing the interviewee squarely and presenting yourself symbolically as a threat. It is preferable that there be no obstruction between participants other than the corner of a desk. You can lean back or forward in your chair, depending on the context of the interview. However, avoid leaning your chair back against a wall, and don't put your feet up on the desk. Keep your body position alert, and project an attentive, professional appearance at all times.

Begin the interview with yourself and the interviewee in the conversation location. Be careful not to violate the interviewee's personal space. If you go past that invisible line and step into the interviewee's "flight area," she will probably back off to increase the space between you. The interviewee's flight area is located somewhere within the moderate location.

The Moderate Location

The *moderate location* brings interview participants to within about four feet of one another, as shown in Figures 10.3 and 10.4. This is close enough to allow the investigator to gently touch the interviewee's arm or shoulder if appropriate. In the moderate location, participants are generally situated at a 45-degree angle, as in the conversation location. At this distance, legs can be crossed carefully. Most interviews and many interrogations can be conducted from the moderate location.

The Intimate Locations

In the first *intimate location*, the participants are situated about two feet apart, as shown in Figures 10.5 and 10.6. As the intensity of the interview increases, the interviewer moves into the second intimate location, to within about a

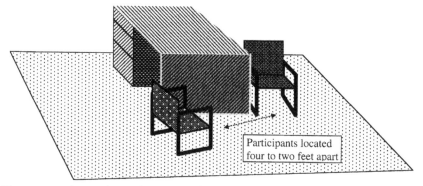

Participants located four to two feet apart

Figure 10.3 The moderate location. The investigator gradually and inconspicuously moves closer to the interviewee until they are about four feet apart.

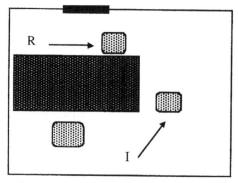

Figure 10.4 Overhead view of a typical interview room, 10 by 12 feet, showing participants in the moderate location. *I* = interviewer; *R* = respondent.

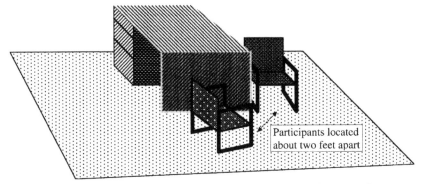

Figure 10.5 The first intimate location. Participants are seated about two feet apart.

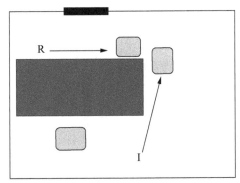

Figure 10.6 Overhead view of a typical interview room, 10 by 12 feet, showing participants in the first intimate location. *I* = interviewer; *R* = respondent.

foot of the interviewee and facing him, as shown in Figures 10.7 and 10.8. The intimate locations may be the most stressful or the most reassuring, depending on how the interview is conducted. In these locations, you can easily reach the interviewee. Your chair is situated quite close to the interviewee's chair so that your knee is next to the interviewee's knee. In this position, the crossing of legs is next to impossible. This distance is reserved for in-depth interviews requiring intense interpersonal communication, great empathy, and lots of encouragement. It is also used for interrogations in which an admission or a confession is sought.

The investigator's shift in position from intimate location 1 to intimate location 2 often accompanies a change in the interview strategy, from resolving inconsistencies (interviewing) to attempting to gain an admission or a confession (interrogating). The successful investigator will make this transition smoothly, not only in shifting position, but also in the comments,

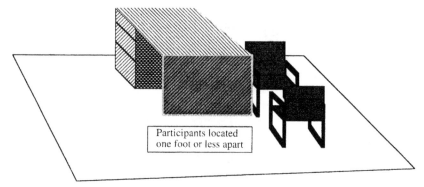

Figure 10.7 The second intimate location. Participants are seated about one foot apart.

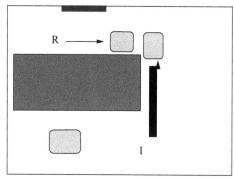

Figure 10.8 Overhead view of a typical interview room, 10 feet by 12 feet, showing participants in the second intimate location. *I*= interviewer; *R*= respondent.

questions, and intensity she employs. In the intimate locations, the rhetorical questions and statements used differ from the investigator's previous efforts to assist the interviewee to rationalize and save face.

REVIEW AND ENCOURAGEMENT INTENSITIES

Throughout the interview, you need to review the facts of the case and their implications with the interviewee and encourage him to answer questions truthfully. Using verbal and nonverbal communication, your goal is to persuade the interviewee to reveal information or to make an admission or a confession. The intensity of this review and encouragement varies throughout the different stages of the interview process. The objective of using varying degrees of intensity is to bring out verbal and nonverbal signals that indicate that the interviewee is lying. *Intensity*, the amount of effort put into making the investigator's presentation remarkable or powerful, is signaled by the investigator's total presentation: how and where the participants are seated; the investigator's tone of voice, facial expressions, and body language; and the investigator's questions and comments and how they are formulated.

Review

The topics you choose to review with the interviewee vary with the phases of the interview, as does the intensity of that review. From general to more specific, the investigator's level of review might increase as follows:

- Inquiry into the circumstances of the matter under investigation.
- Discussion regarding the interviewee's knowledge, opportunity, access, and motivation as they relate to the matter under investigation.
- Consideration of the totality of the circumstances in lesser or greater depth.
- Consideration of the interviewee's relationship to the totality of the circumstances, with less or more focus.
- Coverage of the totality of the circumstances as related to the interviewee's knowledge, opportunity, access, and motivation.

Encouragement

The reason to encourage the interviewee is to reassure him or her and to reach a certain objective, which is the *truth*. During the process of trying to reach that goal, only positive methods to encourage the interviewee to tell the truth are suggested:

- Persuading
- Selling
- Influencing
- Calling for the truth

The use of review and encouragement does not involve bullying, threatening, coercing, or punishing the interviewee.

Intensity Levels

Now let's look at each intensity level and illustrate the specific kinds of review and encouragement that operate at each level.

Level One

Level one, representing general review and minimal encouragement, is used in all interviews from point A to between points C and D on the polyphasic flowchart (refer back to Figure 9.1). At this level, the least amount of effort is employed in using review and encouragement. No attempt is made to point out gaps or inconsistencies in the interviewee's story. Level one is also used for the preliminary inquiry during the precontact section of the initial phase. While obtaining details regarding the matter under investigation, it isn't appropriate to challenge the information provided. There will be a time for that later, if necessary.

Level Two

Level two, used from between points C and D to point F on the flowchart, represents the greatest amount of general review and minimal encouragement. Compared to level one, in this level there is more effort to use these tools. No gaps in the interviewee's story are pointed out or challenged, but some effort is made to clarify details. The "bones" discussed in Chapter 9 are used to draw out the truth. At this intensity level, interviewees may, through verbal and nonverbal signs, indicate that they are trying to dodge your questions or are providing dishonest answers.

Level Three

Used between points F and I of the flowchart, intensity level three involves specific review and persistent encouragement. At this level, the interviewer discusses any inconsistencies that he noted earlier in the interview. This is not a time to interrogate but rather a time to revisit investigative detail. The interviewer must be bold enough to state clearly that there are inconsistencies that must be resolved. The investigator tries to persuade the interviewee that it is inevitable that the truth will eventually be discovered.

During this level, culpable interviewees will probably reveal further signs of their deception. Then it is time for the interviewer to take on the role of interrogator and look for an admission or a confession. The interviewer puts on a different hat, so to speak, becoming assertive and more determined. Between points H and I of the interview process, the interrogator begins to sell the subject on the idea of telling the truth to "get this thing cleared up." Having taken this road, the interrogator cannot back down—unless he becomes convinced that it's the wrong direction.

Don't rush to use intensity level three with interviewees as soon as you notice inconsistencies. Make it a general rule to tune in to inconsistencies during the primary phase without pouncing on interviewees because of them. Throughout the interview, gradually focus attention on the inconsistencies and become more assertive in pointing out gaps in the interviewee's story. Become less accepting of excuses while you begin to challenge the patterns of deception. Sell the interviewee on the idea of willingly divulging the truth.

Level Four

Level four, used between points I and K on the flowchart, represents a greater intensity of specific review and persistent encouragement than level three. Sometimes even the victim is found to be lying and is then interrogated. Most interviewees never reach this level of interaction, however, because the investigator decides that they are being truthful. Remember that it is a mistake to interrogate everyone as though they were guilty or deceptive. Level four reaches its greatest intensity between points J and K as the interrogator attempts to gain an admission or a confession. (A *confession* includes several significant incriminatory statements, whereas an *admission* is one or more incriminatory statements of a more minor nature.) This level of intensity includes greater efforts to help the subject rationalize and save face while she confesses total or partial responsibility for the matter under investigation.

Level Five

Level five is used between points K and M on the flowchart. It represents about the same intensity of specific review and persistent encouragement as in level four; however, level five represents more effort by the investigator in reviewing and encouraging more focus of energy and determination. The interrogator moves closer to the subject while showing a greater degree of certainty that the subject committed the crime. More persuasion is used in level five to sell the subject on the idea to confess. By this point in the interrogation, your subject may have provided an admission but not a complete confession. At point L, the investigator decides whether to ask the subject to undergo a detection-of-deception examination to confirm the supposedly limited nature of her involvement.

APPROACHES

The interview process outlined in this book involves three approaches built around the kinds of questions asked. These three approaches—the structured, semistructured, and nonstructured approaches—are illustrated in the polyphasic flowchart in Chapter 9 (refer back to Figure 9.1).

The Structured Approach

The *structured approach* is used at the beginning of the interview and forms the baseline for the investigator's direct observation, evaluation, and assessment of the interviewee. This approach begins at point A of the flowchart and ends between points C and D. In this portion of the interview, the investigator asks basic fact-finding questions without accusation or intimidation. These questions require less deep thought from the interviewee than those asked during the semistructured and nonstructured modes. To encourage the interviewee to respond, ask questions that she can answer easily. For this purpose, I use routine questions such as the spelling of the interviewee's name, the number of years of schooling, and the type of work done in the past.

The questions asked in the structured approach are not directly related to solving the investigative problem. Instead they give the interviewee an opportunity to evaluate the investigator and to determine whether he will be treated fairly. Everything the investigator does sends a signal to the interviewee. Every part of the investigator's presentation encourages or discourages cooperation. Certainly, if the interviewee is hostile by nature to everyone in authority or is determined to lie, little of what you do and say during the interview will make any difference. Often, however, you can nudge reluctant interviewees into a more compliant stance and eventually even nurture the guilty party into a position to admit or confess to the incident.

At first, you can expect some delay in the interviewee's responses. Do not automatically consider this to be a significant indication of potential deception. Note how clearly the interviewee answers the question; this will help you determine the interviewee's ability to handle more complex questions later in the interview. The structured portion of the interview is the time to begin building rapport with the interviewee. The structured approach can help establish the relative status of the interview participants and assist in creating a secure feeling for both.

The Semistructured Approach

The semistructured approach begins at about point C of the flowchart. The use of this approach implies your desire to receive information from interviewees in an immediate way—that is, promptly and without rambling.

However, it does not imply the use of coercion, abuse, or intimidation. Accusation and confrontation toward interviewees is not appropriate in this mode. With the semistructured approach, try to tune into what is happening moment by moment. You should be alert for signs that the truth is trying to show itself. Look for patterns signaling deception.

The formulation of questions in the semistructured mode is not materially altered by the interviewee's responses. The questions are partly intended to stimulate the interviewee to exhibit verbal and nonverbal behavior that may be indicative of deception. Follow the "bones" described in Chapter 9 in formulating your questions.

The Nonstructured Approach

At about point F or G of the interview interaction, you may decide to alter your interview strategy and use specific review and persistent encouragement to resolve inconsistencies in the interviewee's story. You will usually reach a strategic deduction while attempting to resolve inconsistencies. The interviewee's hostility or reluctance to provide truthful information might be the basis for a greater intensity of review and encouragement. This turning point requires delicate handling. If you decide prematurely that the interviewee is being deceptive and change your strategy abruptly, you might spark greater reluctance on the part of the interviewee. Between points F and H, after attempting to resolve inconsistencies, you may decide to clearly proclaim your belief in the interviewee's culpability and to begin an interrogation. Proficient interrogators move smoothly and cleverly to help the interviewee reveal the truth.

PUTTING IT ALL TOGETHER

There is a clear relationship among the levels of intensity, the participant locations, and the three approaches used during the interview process. During the first part of the interview, the investigator simultaneously uses the structured approach and the level-one intensity stage. As he begins to use the semistructured approach, the intensity increases to level two. Finally, as the investigator attempts to resolve inconsistencies in the interviewee's story, he employs the nonstructured approach and intensity levels three, four, and five.

When the participants are in the conversation location, the approach ranges from structured to semistructured. Touching does not occur. The intensity of review and encouragement stays in the general and minimal ranges.

In the moderate location, intensity levels one, two, and three are used. The distance between the interview participants varies with the intensity of the interaction. When using levels one and two, the investigator maintains a distance of about four feet from the interviewee. With level three, the distance between participants is about four feet. From points C to G on the polyphasic flowchart (refer back to Figure 9.1), the participants are about four feet apart; from G to J, two to four feet; and from J to K, about two feet. Reassuring touch is not used with levels one and two, but it can be employed with level three at a distance of about two feet. In the moderate location, the semistructured and nonstructured approaches are used to formulate questions. Between points F and G, the investigator might announce that there appear to be inconsistencies in the information that the interviewee has provided.

The intimate location is used with intensity level four. The investigator uses this location to comfort or confront. *Intimate* implies closeness between participants that might strengthen rapport and stimulate greater cooperation. Confrontations about inconsistencies take place in this location, as do the beginnings of interrogation.

REVIEW QUESTIONS

1. What is a key consideration in selecting an interview location?
2. What is personal space, and what might happen if you invade an interviewee's personal space?
3. What is proxemics, and why is it important?
4. What are the three locations, and how are they used in the interview process?
5. Name two uses for the intimate locations.
6. How can you use review and encouragement strategically to uncover the truth?
7. What is the objective of using the various intensity levels of review and encouragement?
8. Is it appropriate to use tactics involving bullying or coercion at the highest intensity level?
9. When should you challenge inconsistencies?
10. What is the goal of the structured approach, and what types of questions are appropriate?
11. When is the semistructured approach used?
12. When does a turning point in strategy occur?

CHAPTER 11

Questioning Techniques

Interviewing is best done face to face. In the complex interaction that takes place during an interview, observations are made by both participants as they check and recheck each other's verbal and nonverbal behavior. There is a mutual analysis: The interviewee is scrutinizing the investigator for signs of believability while being observed for patterns of deception. Seasoned interviewers know that luck is merely what is left over after careful planning and preparation. They develop a plan for each interview but remain flexible when applying it. They help interviewees rationalize and save face, thus encouraging their cooperation.

It is worth remembering that when someone is being interviewed, she is likely going to undergo stress, even if in minimal amounts. As difficult as it may be for you, finding a way to portray yourself as kind and gentle may pay off with big rewards. It is important to be empathetic while remaining curious and interviewing with purpose. Your questions need to be objective, thorough, relevant, and accurate. Proficient interviewers have a keen sense of observation, resourcefulness, and persistence as well as a tireless capacity for work. They also use common sense. Acting stern, imperious, or harsh will not help your interview. Be guided by your intuition, not guesses or speculations, but be sure your intuition is based on your direct observation and immediate experience. Be prepared to interview without conveying pressure or suggestion, and encourage the interviewee to provide a narrative account of their statement. Ask the interviewee to recall everything related to this particular case, observed or known. It is always better to interview witnesses as soon as possible after an incident, so that they can give a more accurate report.

Interviewing and interviewing techniques have changed tremendously over the past 10 years, specifically in regard to the way witnesses and suspects are interviewed. Years ago interviews were primarily confrontational, whereas now we hope to get the interviewee to be cooperative, producing a meaningful interview.

Unobtrusively direct the interview, deciding when to listen, when to talk, what to observe, and so on. In so doing, observe, evaluate, and assess the interviewees, including what they say both verbally and nonverbally, how they say what they say, and what they fail to say. The plausibility of a witness's observation is critical to the overall investigation; therefore, consider the ability of each interviewee to see and hear what was reportedly observed. With overly talkative interviewees who ramble or with those who tend to wander from the topic, gently and empathically guide them back, redirecting them through leading questions to a discussion of the issue at hand.

Interviewees provide opinions wherever and whenever they can; it is your job to distinguish true factual information from opinionated, emotional comments. Separate observations from interpretations, facts from feelings. If you notice interviewees interpreting facts rather than presenting observed details, avoid being judgmental and pouncing on them. Without pressure or suggestion, encourage them to provide a narrative of their observations regarding the investigative problem. Avoid knowingly bringing into your inquiry any biases or prejudices that might lead to misguided observations and improper evaluation.

QUESTION FORMULATION

Interviewers succeed when they convince their subjects to provide truthful information. It's not a matter of *telling* but rather of *selling*. Well-crafted questions can sell the interviewee on the idea of telling the truth. You need to be a persuader of sorts, using properly phrased questions in a setting and under circumstances that persuade the interviewee to answer honestly. Questions encourage compliance when their design is simple. Make them more specific and complex only after evaluating the interviewee's responses. Aristotle said, "Think as wise men do, but speak as the common people do." Ask questions spontaneously to express ideas in a natural and subconscious manner. Trust yourself to ask properly worded questions while encouraging the subject to cooperate. When appropriate, make your questions specific, definite, and concrete. Vague, general questions permit interviewees to wiggle and squirm away from your desired goal.

Choose your words with care. Words represent partial images, not the total picture. Avoid legal-sounding terms like *homicide*, *assault*, and *embezzlement*. Misused, these words tend to make interviewees unnecessarily defensive. Interviewees welcome the opportunity to respond to questions for which they know the answers, and they feel freer to talk when the topic is familiar. Interview suspects tend to avoid answering questions that make them appear dumb, foolish, or uninformed. When embarrassed or upset over a question, interviewees avoid eye contact and may display signs of distress. Some people appear shifty-eyed when they are lying, are planning to lie, or have been asked to reveal private information about themselves.

QUESTION PRESENTATION

A question is a direct or implied request for the interviewee to think about a particular matter. Comments based on assumptions can be regarded as questions if they invite the interviewee to respond. Rather than rely on many questions, allow the interviewee to speak freely. Some interviewees elaborate more readily when asked fewer questions. Once an interviewee decides to talk, you often need only guide the discussion with timely encouragement. Your assumptions, behavior, and method of questioning will, to some extent, determine the interviewee's response and willingness to cooperate. Even your vocabulary could cause embarrassment or fright. Interviewees who lose face because they don't understand your words may become disturbed or insulted, they may feel naked and vulnerable, and they may become judgmental and skeptical (Berne, 1974; Harris, 1973; *I Understand, You Understand*). Their resentment may cause them to fail to think clearly, to refuse to cooperate, or even to lie. On the other hand, some interviewees will be extremely cooperative in trying to answer all questions, even with an interviewer who asks poorly phrased questions based on crude, biased assumptions. By initiating the question- answer pattern, you tell interviewees as plainly as if put into words that you are the authority, the expert, and that only you know what is important and relevant. This may humiliate some interviewees who regard such a pattern as a third-degree tactic. Therefore, phrase your questions carefully, and be sensitive enough to realize when not to ask questions. Noticing the sincerity of your tone of questioning and how you avoid asking abrasive, leading questions, interviewees will feel less need to be defensive.

Question objectively. Avoid giving the impression that you have taken sides in the investigation. This may be difficult for interviewers who represent certain organizations, such as law enforcement agencies. Avoid looking surprised or shocked at any statement an interviewee makes.

Regard the interview as a conversation, not a cross-examination. "Do not grill the interviewee as a prosecuting attorney might do. Ask questions in a conversational manner, because your purpose is to hold a conversation with someone who has knowledge or has experienced something that you want to know about. Holding a conversation implies a certain amount of give-and-take during the interview. Your goal is to ask questions that are productive, yielding information. Try to avoid making statements that do not illicit an answer.

Never ask questions in a belligerent, demeaning, or sarcastic manner. Questions that begin "Isn't it true that you ..." tend to be abrasive and promote defensiveness. Pushing interviewees into a corner where they will have to defend themselves is self-defeating. Do not embarrass interviewees by asking questions that they cannot answer. This will only make them uneasy and will create unnecessary tension. Similarly, asking questions accusingly, suspiciously, or abruptly or asking "trick questions" may arouse fear and defensiveness and will not promote cooperation. All of these tactics are counterproductive.

To emphasize your genuine interest in the details the interviewee has provided and to promote a positive view of your thoroughness, review all details during questioning. This will allow coverage of more specific areas of interest as the need arises. Make it appear that some details are not as clear as they could be, or claim to have missed some meaningful information.

TYPES OF QUESTIONS

Two main types of questions are generally used in interviews: closed questions and open questions. The objective of the inquiry determines the use of closed or open questions. Fewer tactical restrictions apply to using open questions. By tactical restrictions, I mean strategic limitations that might hamper your progress in calling for the truth. Open questions allow for various angles or degrees of considered approach. They can be calculated to emphasize points of the inquiry using various levels of review and encouragement.

Closed Questions

Closed, or *closed-ended*, questions are specific, offering a limited number of possible responses. Yes-or-no questions and multiple-choice questions are types of closed questions. These types of questions are also risky because they don't allow the interviewee to communicate freely. Often times, closed-ended questions are counterproductive and limit rapport building. If used, ask them at the beginning of an interview to encourage affirmative responses and to put interviewees more at ease. Used later in the interview, closed questions will limit your efforts to reveal information.

The yes-no or either-or option of some closed questions limits the scope of responses and options. This can be useful when you want to maintain maximum control over the interview and thereby save some time. They are also handy when dealing with reluctant interviewees who will not give detailed responses. To gain information, narrow [closed] questions have the advantage of eliciting details. Open-ended questions rely on the [interviewee's] ability to recall. However, the unrestricted use of closed questions will hamper your efforts. "Narrow questions can inhibit the development of rapport. . . . The misuse of narrow questions involves detailed probing before the [interviewee] is ready. People will be willing to provide details, particularly about sensitive subjects, only if they feel comfortable in doing so. Therefore, probing too soon, without first having developed a rapport, may cause the interviewee to feel improperly invaded".[1]

Open Questions

Open, or *open-ended,* questions start with *who, where, what, when, how,* or *why.* They cannot be answered yes or no, and they require the suspect to think clearly. Although they create the most distress, they also reveal the greatest amount of information. These questions are also the most productive ones. Open questions help interviews flow. Most open questions ask *what, why,* or *how.*

To learn the cause, reasons, or purpose, ask the question *why. Why* questions search out the facts of a situation and probe areas not commonly touched by more complicated questions. There are times, however, when the *why* question creates a threatening situation in which interviewees become defensive. Faced with the question "Why?" they may feel rejected, misunderstood, or imposed upon. They may withdraw, prevaricate, or hit back with silence that may confuse or frustrate you. Questions beginning with *why* may provoke undue stress because they generate too much challenge. Interviewees generally cannot answer the question "Why?" regarding subconscious thinking or behavior. Answering reveals too much of the self, and self-disclosure makes people uncomfortable.

Open questions can help you accomplish several goals:

- Discover the interviewee's priorities, attitudes, needs, values, aims, and aspirations.
- Determine the interviewee's frame of reference and viewpoints.
- Establish empathic understanding and rapport.
- Engage in active listening, stroking, positive regard, and recognition.
- Allow and encourage interviewees to express their feelings and reveal facts without feeling threatened.
- Promote catharsis or expression of the interviewee's emotions.

Several different types of open questions can be used effectively during an interview. Anticipating the impact of each question that you ask will help you formulate them. Open question types are discussed in the following sections.

---

[1] Binder and Price, 1977, pp. 44–45.

Reflective Questions

Reflective questions mirror the subject's comments. They are used to handle objections. You might begin, "Let me see if I've got this straight . . ." or "So, what you're saying is . . .." Once you've responded to the interviewee's concerns, repeat the question that triggered the objection. By removing the obstacle to cooperation, you help the interviewee feel more comfortable responding to your subsequent questions.

Directive Questions

Directive questions are used to direct the interviewee's attention to areas of agreement with the investigator. Interviewees want to know the benefits to themselves of cooperation. A directive question answers this concern: "You do want to get to the bottom of this, don't you?"

Pointed Questions

Pointed, or *direct, questions* are detailed and specific in nature, pointing directly at the goal. Pointed questions are complex and persuasive. They are designed to rouse the interviewee to action. Most of the questions asked in forensic interviews are pointed questions. By asking exactly what is desired, you show interviewees that you believe they are ready, willing, and able to respond. This method, which is based on the self-fulfilling prophecy, works most of the time.

Pointed questions might stimulate the physical expression of the interviewee's stress, but they need not be offensive or accusatory. On the contrary, they should be thoughtfully developed and subtly applied to avoid invoking stress and making the subject defensive. You can gently stimulate the interviewee's thinking with pointed, creative questions. For example, if you believe that the interviewee accidentally set a fire, you might ask, "On the day of the fire, how often did you smoke in the break room?"

Indirect Questions

Pointed questions are not always appropriate. *Indirect questions* provoke less stress, less fear, and hence less defensiveness on the part of the interviewee. They help subjects save face and rationalize their behavior by giving them "a universal blessing." For example, you might say, "I've talked to many of the other employees, and they believe that. . . What do you think?" Indirect questions of this nature can help interviewees express their hidden selves, their thoughts and feelings, and so on. Indirect questions are often used at the beginning of an interview and as a change of pace during the course of the discussion. They can also be used as diversion questions (see the discussion that follows).

Self-Appraisal Questions

Self-appraisal questions ask the interviewee to evaluate or judge himself. They help the investigator develop a hypothesis about the *who, how,* and *why* of a crime or another incident. Through self-appraisal questions, the interviewer gains a deeper understanding of the interviewee's needs and probes his opinion, revealing possible evasiveness and distress. It is almost impossible for a deceptive or evasive interviewee to be consistent in answering self-appraisal questions. To respond deceptively, the interviewee must first think of an answer, decide that the answer would not sound good, and then make up a new story and tell it convincingly.

Diversion Questions

Diversion questions focus on something or someone near and dear to the interviewee. They have two purposes: (1) They lessen tension by distracting the interviewee from a tension-producing issue, and (2) they restore rapport between the subject and the investigator with a direct or indirect compliment. Diversion questions are useful when dealing with highly emotional interviewees. For example, the investigator might say in a matter-of-fact tone, "Now, let's put that aside for a minute. I want to cover another point with you about your view of how the company can improve the security. As I mentioned, part of why I'm interviewing several people is to accomplish two things. First, I would like to get that missing money back and second, I want to prevent this from happening again. Let me ask you, how can such a loss be prevented in the future?" The rambling nature of the question provides time for the interviewee to calm down if the interviewer had pushed some emotional buttons in previous questions.

Leading Questions

Leading questions include some assumption on the part of the investigator. For example, the statement "From what I hear you say, you must have had a rough time in that job last summer" contains an assumption and invites the interviewee to elaborate or explain. Leading questions containing implicit messages can be used to maintain moderate emotional tension in the interview, but they need not be abrasive if thoughtfully constructed. Leading questions can guide the interviewee toward greater cooperation with your investigation. They reflect your assumption that the interviewee can provide useful information. Leading questions can convey the interviewer's acceptance of the individual, thereby enhancing rapport.

Leading questions are usually thought to produce invalid, unreliable answers. This is true when they are carelessly used. Novice investigators sometimes have trouble using leading questions because their tone of voice and related nonverbal signals are not well controlled. Consequently, interviewees may feel condemned when faced with carelessly presented leading questions. Ulterior motives are typically built into leading questions. Use leading questions with the ulterior motive of stimulating conversation and encouraging the interviewee to reveal the truth.

TECHNIQUES FOR EFFECTIVE QUESTIONING

The following guidelines will help you formulate effective interview questions:

- Avoid the third degree.
- Use closed questions when appropriate.
- Use open questions when appropriate.
- Keep your questions simple.
- Avoid ambiguously worded questions.
- Use leading questions properly.
- Ask self-appraisal questions.
- Have the gall to ask tough questions.
- Encourage cooperation.
- Mentally assume an affirmative answer.
- Pursue unanswered questions.
- Identify and challenge deception.
- Handle trial balloons calmly.
- Assume more information is available.

Having the Gall to Ask

Investigators sometimes have problems asking tough or embarrassing questions, and they may even avoid asking these questions to save themselves from embarrassment. There is no doubt it takes a certain amount of gall to ask someone if he stole the money or killed the wife. Conducting an investigative interview requires that you be brave enough to ask questions that would be rude and intrusive in other situations. As a skilled interviewer, you will know when and how to ask the hard questions.

Encouraging Cooperation

If an interviewee has a role in an investigation, it is one of assisting the investigator by providing information that she alone may have. Encourage interviewees to provide information even when they might not understand what their role is in the investigation. The investigator collects information picked up by the interviewee who may have seen or heard something of value to the inquiry. Intentionally altering your verbal and nonverbal communication in a positive manner may stimulate your interviewee to be cooperative and truthful. Encourage her to feel that cooperation enhances her sense of usefulness.

When interviewees try to argue that they should not comply, they are indicating that they are at least considering compliance or they wouldn't argue the point. Even interviewees who show up for a scheduled interview and sit quietly without responding to questions signal that they are considering compliance. Assume that reluctant interviewees have some degree of resentment, and ask questions designed to uncover that hidden resentment. An interviewer's concerned attempts to convey compassion to a victim may be enough to encourage someone to share needed information. That someone may be the interviewee's friend or relative who learns of the attempt at compassion.

Refusal tends to be the most resistant response from uncooperative interviewees. The interviewee may decide to cooperate in the future. If interviewees sense that they can leave if they choose, they often start trusting the interviewer. Their freedom to leave tends to release any fear that might hinder compliance.

Although most interviewees feel a personal obligation to answer truthfully, that obligation is lessened when the investigator is obviously unskilled in formulating questions. If the interviewee's expectations conflict with the investigator's questioning style, the interviewee may feel frustrated or annoyed. Rapport needs to be a developed in order to encourage cooperation.

Interviewee reluctance or hostility may indicate avoidance of the topic under investigation, fear of retaliation, or maybe personal involvement in the delinquency. Your task is to guide the subject toward cooperation, convincing her to cooperate. If and when the interviewee feels a sense of obligation, she will provide you with information. If necessary, help the interviewee create a temporary new identity that will allow her to move from limited compliance to more complete cooperation. Such tactics are not negative if your intentions are basically helpful and honorable.

You can encourage cooperation by beginning the interview with simple closed questions that invite a positive response before asking more complex, specific, open questions. By conveying the impression that you need and expect additional facts, you can subtly encourage the interviewee to reveal more information. If you can do so without creating unnecessary tension, imply that you have already obtained considerable information against which you will check the interviewee's responses.

Mentally Assuming an Affirmative Answer

Uncooperative interviewees are willing to terminate an interview as soon as comfortably possible, particularly if they sense that you doubt your own abilities to obtain information. All they need is some encouragement in the form of negatively phrased questions, such as, "You wouldn't happen to know anything about the fire, would you?" Investigators typically shake their head from side to side when asking questions such as this one.

To avoid receiving negative responses that lead you to a dead end, mentally assume an affirmative answer to a closed question and ask the next logical question instead. For example, don't ask, "Have you seen or talked with Sam Smith recently?" The interviewee could define recently as "within the last several hours" and could answer no, closing off further discussion. Instead, assume that the interviewee *has* seen Smith recently and ask, "When was the last time you saw or talked with Sam Smith?"

This second question, an open question, cannot be answered yes or no. The interviewee must give a complete response if he answers at all. The response you receive will determine the direction of subsequent questions. For example, if the interviewee responds, "I spoke with Sam two days ago," you might ask, "What was Sam wearing when you last saw him? What kind of car was he driving? Who was he hanging around with?" These questions will help you determine Smith's appearance, his means of transportation, and his current associates.

Pursuing Unanswered Questions

There are many reasons why an interviewee might fail to answer a question or might provide an incomplete or nonsensical response. Perhaps the interviewee is preoccupied or distracted and did not hear the question correctly, or perhaps he is too overwhelmed by emotion to answer. If your question was poorly worded, the interviewee might not have understood what you were asking. Be patient. Give the interviewee time to think without challenging him. Then ask the question again, varying the wording if appropriate. Never ignore an unanswered question to go on to another topic. To go on and leave questions unanswered will only cause you eventual frustration.

Of course, the interviewee might ignore a question because she has something to hide. Always maintain a certain amount of unexpressed skepticism. When repeating a question, be alert for possible signals of deception. Be aware of patterns indicating that the truth is emerging. By not answering, an innocent interviewee might hope to avoid discussion of a difficult topic. You can reduce tension by repeating or rewording your question. When the interview touches on sensitive or threatening topics, you may need to restate a question to find a more acceptable form. Some words trigger mental images that may be emotionally painful to the interviewee, causing her to block out certain thoughts. Whether you repeat or reword a question depends on the circumstances and how you evaluate your progress in the interview.

There are times when it is useful to ask a mild, modified version of an emotionally loaded question before asking the main question. This warns the interviewee of the emotional question to follow, helping the interviewee prepare for it. At other times, it is necessary to spring emotion-laden questions on the interviewee to reveal any hidden tension.

Never demand an answer to a question. Don't point out that the interviewee failed to answer. Instead, reword your question and try again. Some interviewees will try to provoke you into challenging them so they will feel justified in storming out of the interview room. Even victims and witnesses of a crime may feel insulted if challenged by a demand to answer a question. By calmly repeating your questions, you signal persistence, patience, and humanity, which strengthen the bonds of interpersonal communication.

Identifying and Challenging Deception

Although we cannot claim King Solomon's special wisdom, we can at least use our talents as observers to uncover the truth. We can watch for behavioral patterns that indicate possible deception.

A lead-in that introduces a change of topic—for example, "Now I'm going to ask you a few questions about the day the money was missing"—causes some interviewees to nonverbally signal their intent to deceive. They may fidget in their chair, cross their legs or arms, or break eye contact. Any such sign of uneasiness should cause you to question mentally the truthfulness of the answers that follow.

Do not immediately confront or challenge interviewees who display signs of uneasiness prior to or while answering announced questions. To challenge indicates that you have concluded that the topic of the question is bothersome or that the interviewee intends to lie. Instead, ask your question, and note the interviewee's uneasiness for review later. Look for patterns of evasiveness that may indicate deception. When a clear pattern of evasiveness becomes evident, gradually challenge the interviewee. Isolated signs of evasiveness, although important, are not enough to warrant a challenge.

Some degree of unprovoked anxiety may be useful in an interview. *Unprovoked anxiety* means an uneasiness brought to the interview and not caused by the investigator as some planned effort. That anxiety may be caused by the interviewee's knowledge of someone's personal responsibility. When you sense unprovoked anxiety, you can use it as the basis for displaying your humanity and showing you are okay to talk to. You can enhance tension through your use of questions or by commenting about the interviewee's defense mechanisms or sensitivity to certain events. However, insensitive confrontation over conflicting details in the interviewee's story could cause undue tension, evasiveness, and defensiveness, resulting in an unproductive interview.

Handling Trial Balloons

Interviewees sometimes ask *trial balloon* questions. For example, a subject might ask, "Let's say I did take the money—what would happen to me?" or "What usually happens to a person who steals merchandise?" These *what-if* questions may indicate that the interviewee is on the brink of reporting some significant fact.

When the interviewee floats a trial balloon, avoid pouncing on it as an admission of guilt. Instead, calmly respond to the inquiry, and subtly ask questions that encourage the interviewee to tell the truth. What-if questions are used to test the water, so to speak, to see if it is safe. They signal the need for continued patience and persistence; they do not indicate that it is time to charge ahead destructively.

Terminating the Interview

Always assume that more information is forthcoming and that you need only ask appropriate questions and give adequate encouragement. Even when it seems you have reached the termination point—when it seems as though all questions have been asked and answered—continue to assume that the interviewee has more to tell you. You might ask, "What else can you tell me about what happened?" or "What else should I know about this matter?"

At some point, of course, you will need to terminate the interview. You can do this several ways. Even if you have no intention of questioning the subject again, you might announce that a second interview is possible. Or you might make arrangements for a second interview and give yourself time to further prepare. Finally, you might lead into a confrontation by announcing that you believe there are inconsistencies that must be resolved or by specifically accusing the interviewee of the crime. Your next step would be to attempt to gain a confession or an admission of guilt. In most instances, you will probably end the interview and not need to speak with that person again.

CONCLUSION

On a final note, take the recent interview of the 2013 Boston Marathon bomber. The second bomber had been captured and was interviewed for the first time. Reports stated that he had been shot in the throat and couldn't speak. Assume that you are instructed to conduct the interview and you need to be prepared and ready for a series of questions that you need to address immediately, knowing that he will likely stop talking once he is given his Miranda warning. Remember that the right questions could prevent future mass casualties and mass destruction.

REVIEW QUESTIONS

1. What is the objective of interviewing?
2. How can leading questions help you with overly talkative interviewees?
3. How should you respond when the interviewee provides opinions instead of facts?
4. Why shouldn't you ask vague questions?
5. What is a question?
6. Why is it important to ask questions objectively?
7. Is the interview a conversation or a cross-examination? Explain.
8. Give two examples of closed questions.
9. How do most open questions begin?
10. What are two things that open questions can help you do?
11. Name three types of open questions, and give an example of each.
12. How are pointed questions based on the self-fulfilling prophecy?
13. What type of question can help you develop and strengthen rapport?

14. What is one advantage of using leading questions?
15. How do polite social conversations differ from investigative interviews?
16. How does your expectation play a role in gaining truthful information?
17. Why isn't it a good idea to ignore unanswered questions and go on with the interview?
18. How might your questions trigger emotions that block the interviewee's thought process?
19. What is a trial balloon question, and how should you respond to it?
20. Why should you assume that the interviewee has more to tell you, even at the end of the interview?

CHAPTER 12

Internal Investigations and Controls

If you are an investigator working for a corporation, security firm, retail organization, insurance company, or private client, you will likely find yourself conducting interviews for the purpose of securing a confession to a criminal offense. Our role often starts with preliminary research, moves into an investigation, and finally leads into an interview for the purpose of obtaining a statement or confession. I have spent much of the past 35 years conducting corporate investigations into fraud, embezzlement, drug use, theft, and other wrongdoings. These investigations have taken anywhere from hours to more than six months. You will need to exercise patience in conducting internal investigation cases; however, it has been my experience that once an employee is successfully (that is, not being caught) stealing or committing fraud, they continue to do so. The manner in which they commit the crime may change, but their greed doesn't subside.

Depending on the state laws and company laws, you may need several conclusive videos in which the criminal act is being committed prior to conducting your interview.

There are many things to consider when you're conducting internal investigations:

- What was the source that provided initial information and under what terms? (That is, informant, whistleblower, co-conspirator, witness, etc.)
- Determine who might be allowed into the knowledge of an ongoing investigation.
- Who will you want to interview and what information might they have?
- Determine whether the allegations fall under criminal conduct or an internal discipline matter.
- Address any conflicts of interest by anyone connected to the investigation.
- Be prepared to document everything related to this case.
- Who in the company needs to be notified of the investigation? (That is, human resources, legal department, auditing, financial department)
- What evidence will you need to gather to prosecute this case?

- Know and follow all relevant company policies.
- Consider all laws that might apply.

While trying to understand the complexities of internal investigations, let's look at internal theft, dishonest employees, danger signals, and keys to reducing theft.

The remaining text in this chapter is reprinted, with permission, from Chapter 13, "Internal Theft Controls and Personnel Issues," from *Introduction to Security,* ninth edition (Fischer and Halibozek, 2013).

INTRODUCTION

It is sad but true that virtually every company will suffer losses from internal theft—and these losses can be enormous. Early in this new century, even the large corporate giants such as Enron, WorldCom, and Martha Stewart have been affected by internal corruption that reached the highest levels of the organization. In addition, the name Bernie Madoff will long be associated with perhaps the greatest customer and company theft of all times. In its 2010 report, *The Cost of Occupational Fraud,* the Association of Certified Fraud Examiners estimated that fraud (employee theft) cost the world business community $2.9 trillion, or 5% of the estimated gross world product, in 2009. Although this figure is startling, it must be remembered that there is no accurate way to calculate the extent of fraud. In 2002, Security reported that in the retail business alone, 1 in every 27 employees is apprehended for theft from an employer. Internal theft in the retail business outstrips the loss from shoplifting by approximately 7.9 times.

The significance of employee theft is pointed out in a 2010 University of Florida and National Retail Federation Report. Dr. Richard Hollinger, lead author, reported that $14.4 billion was lost to retailers, thanks to thieving employees, down slightly from earlier studies.

WHAT IS HONESTY?

Before considering the issue of dishonest employees, it is helpful to understand the concept of honesty, which is difficult to define. Webster says that honesty is "fairness and straightforwardness of conduct, speech, etc.; integrity; truthfulness; freedom; freedom from fraud." In simple terms, honesty is respect for others and for their property. The concept, however, is relative. According to Charles Carson, "Security must be based on a controlled degree of relative honesty" because no one fulfills the ideal of total honesty. Carson explores relative honesty by asking the following questions:

1. If an error is made in your favor in computing the price of something you buy, do you report it?
2. If a cashier gives you too much change, do you return it?
3. If you found a purse containing money and the owner's identification, would you return the money to the owner if the amount was $1? $10? $100? $1,000?

Honesty is a controllable variable, and how much control is necessary depends on the degree of honesty of each individual. The individual's honesty can be evaluated by assessing the degree of two types of honesty: moral and conditioned. *Moral honesty* is a feeling of responsibility and respect that develops during an individual's formative years; this type of honesty is subconscious. *Conditioned honesty* results from fearing the consequences of being caught; it is a product of reasoning. If an honest act is made without a conscious decision, it is because of moral honesty, but if the act is based on the conscious consideration of consequences, the act results from conditioned honesty.

It is vital to understand these principles because the role of security is to hire employees who have good moral honesty and to condition employees to greater honesty. The major concern is that the job should not tempt an employee into dishonesty.

Carson summarizes his views in the following principles:

- No one is completely honest.
- Honesty is a variable that can be influenced for better or worse.
- Temptation is the father of dishonesty.
- Greed, not need, triggers temptation.

Unfortunately, there is no sure way by which potentially dishonest employees can be recognized. Proper screening procedures can eliminate applicants with unsavory pasts or those who seem unstable and therefore possibly untrustworthy. There are even tests that purport to measure an applicant's honesty index. But tests and employee screening can only indicate potential difficulties. They can screen out the most obvious risks, but they can never truly vouch for the performance of any prospective employee under circumstances of new employment or under changes that may come about in life apart from the job.

The need to carefully screen employees has continued to increase. In today's market, there are many individuals who belong to what has been called the "I Deserve It!" Generation. According to a study by the Josephson Institute for the Advanced Study of Ethics, cheating, stealing, and lying by high school students have continued an upward trend, with youth 18 and younger five times more likely than people over age 50 to hold the belief that lying and cheating are necessary to succeed. The 2008 report showed that 64 percent of U.S. high school students cheated on an exam, 42 percent lied to save money, and 30 percent stole something from a store. The Institute, which conducts nonpartisan ethics programs for the Internal Revenue Service, the Pentagon, and several major media organizations and educators, states that their findings show evidence that a willingness to cheat has become the norm. The 2008 study found that young people believe that ethics and character are important but are cynical about whether a person can be ethical and still succeed.

THE DISHONEST EMPLOYEE

Because there is no fail-safe technique for recognizing the potentially dishonest employee on sight, it is important to try to gain some insight into the reasons that employees may steal. If some rule of thumb could be developed that will help identify the patterns of the potential thief, it would provide some warning for an alert manager.

There is no simple answer to the question of why previously honest people suddenly start to steal from their employers. The mental and emotional processes that lead to this change are complex, and motivation may come from any number of sources.

Some employees steal because of resentment over real or imagined injustice that they blame on management indifference or malevolence. Some feel that they must maintain status and steal to augment their incomes because of financial problems. Some may steal simply to tide themselves over in a genuine emergency. They rationalize the theft by assuring themselves that they will return the money after the current problem is solved. Some simply want to indulge themselves, and many, strangely enough, steal to help others. Alternatively, employees may steal because no one cares, because no one is looking, or because the absence or inadequacy of theft controls eliminates the fear of being caught. Still others may steal simply for excitement.

The Fraud Triangle

A simplified answer to the question of why employees steal is depicted in the fraud triangle. According to this concept, theft occurs when three elements are present:

1. Incentive or motive
2. Attitude/rationalization or desire
3. Opportunity

In simple terms, incentive or motive is a reason to steal. Motives might be the resentment of an employee who feels underpaid or the vengefulness of an employee who has been passed over for promotion. Attitude or desire builds on motive by imagining the satisfaction or gratification that would come from a potential action: "Taking a stereo system would make me feel good, because I always wanted a good stereo system." Opportunity is the absence of barriers that prevent someone from taking an item. Desire and motive are beyond the scope of the loss-prevention manager; opportunity, however, is the responsibility of security.

A high percentage of employee thefts begin with opportunities that are regularly presented to them. If security systems are lax or supervision is indifferent, the temptation to steal items that are improperly secured or unaccountable may be too much to resist by any but the most resolute employee.

Many experts agree that the fear of discovery is the most important deterrent to internal theft. When the potential for discovery is eliminated, theft is bound to follow. Threats of dismissal or prosecution of any employee found stealing are never as effective as the belief that any theft will be discovered by management supervision.

Danger Signs

The root causes of theft are many and varied, but certain signs can indicate that a hazard exists. The conspicuous consumer presents perhaps the most easily identified risk. Employees who habitually or suddenly acquire expensive cars and/or clothes and who generally seem to live beyond their means should be watched. Such persons are visibly extravagant and appear indifferent to the value of money. Even though such employees may not be stealing to support expensive tastes, they are likely to run into financial difficulties through reckless spending. Employees may then be tempted to look beyond their salary checks for ways to support an extravagant lifestyle.

Employees who show a pattern of financial irresponsibility are also a potential risk. Many people are incapable of handling their money. They may do their job with great skill and efficiency, but they are in constant difficulty in their private lives. These people are not necessarily compulsive spenders, nor do they necessarily have expensive tastes. (They probably live quite modestly, since they have never been able to manage their affairs effectively enough to live otherwise.) They are simply people who are unable to come to grips with their own economic realities. Garnishments or inquiries by creditors may identify such employees. If there seems a reason to make one, a credit check might reveal the tangled state of affairs.

Employees caught in a genuine financial squeeze are also possible problems. If they have been hit with financial demands from illnesses in the family or heavy tax liens, they may find the pressures too great to bear. If such a situation comes to the attention of management, counseling is in order. Many companies maintain funds that are designated to make low-interest loans in such cases. Alternatively, some arrangement might be worked out through a credit union. In any event, employees in such extremities need help fast. They should get that help, both as a humane response to their needs and as a means of protecting company assets.

In addition to these general categories, there are specific danger signals that should be noted:

- Gambling on or off premises
- Excessive drinking or signs of other drug use
- Obvious extravagance
- Persistent borrowing
- Requests for advances
- Bouncing personal checks or problems with creditors

What Employees Steal

The employee thief will take anything that may be useful or that has resale value. The thief can get at the company funds in many ways—directly or indirectly—through collusion with vendors, collusion with outside thieves or hijackers, fake invoices, receipting for goods never received, falsifying inventories, payroll padding, false certification of overtime, padded expense accounts, computer records manipulation, overcharging, undercharging, or simply by gaining access to a cash box or company goods.

This is only a sample of the kinds of attacks that can be made on company assets using the systems set up for the operation of the business. It is in these areas that the greatest losses can occur because they are frequently based on a systematic looting of the goods and services in which the company deals and the attendant operational cash flow.

Significant losses do occur, however, in other, sometimes unexpected, areas. Furnishings frequently disappear. In some firms with indifferent traffic control procedures, this kind of theft can be a very real problem. Desks, chairs, computers and other office equipment, paintings, rugs—all can be carried away by the enterprising employee thief.

Office supplies can be another problem if they are not properly supervised. Beyond the anticipated attrition in pencils, paper clips, notepads, and rubber bands, sometimes these materials are stolen in case lots. Many firms that buy their supplies at discount are in fact receiving stolen property. The market in stolen office supplies is a brisk one and is becoming more so as the prices for this merchandise soar.

The office equipment market is another active one, and the inside thief is quick to respond to its needs. Computers always bring a good price, as does equipment used to support high-tech offices.

Personal property is also vulnerable. Office thieves do not make fine distinctions between company property and that of their fellow workers. The company has a very real stake in this kind of theft because personal tragedy and decline in morale follow in its wake.

Although security personnel cannot assume responsibility for losses of this nature because they are not in a position to know about the property involved or to control its handling (and they should so inform all employees), they should make every effort to apprise all employees of the threat. They should further note from time to time the degree of carelessness the staff displays in handling personal property and send out reminders of the potential dangers of loss.

Methods of Theft

A 2007 report by Gaston and Associates reported that the American Management Association believes that 20 percent of business failures were the result of employee dishonesty. In addition, a 2010 report by the Association of Certified Fraud Examiners estimates that 5 percent of total revenue losses for most companies are from employee fraud of some type (*2010 Report to the Nation*, p. 4). Therefore, there is a very real need to examine the shapes that dishonesty frequently takes. There is no way to describe every kind of theft, but some examples may serve to give an idea of the dimensions of the problem:

1. Payroll and personnel employees collaborating to falsify records by the use of nonexistent employees or by retaining terminated employees on the payroll
2. Padding overtime reports and kicking back part of the extra unearned pay to the authorizing supervisor
3. Pocketing unclaimed wages
4. Splitting increased payroll that has been raised on signed, blank checks for use in the authorized signer's absence
5. Maintenance personnel and contract servicepeople in collusion to steal and sell office equipment
6. Receiving clerks and truck drivers in collusion on falsification of merchandise count (extra unaccounted merchandise is fenced)
7. Purchasing agents in collusion with vendors to falsify purchase and payment documents (purchasing agent issues authorization for payment on goods never shipped after forging receipts of shipment)
8. Purchasing agent in collusion with vendor to pay inflated price
9. Mailroom and supply personnel packing and mailing merchandise to themselves for resale
10. Accounts payable personnel paying fictitious bills to an account set up for their own use
11. Taking incoming cash without crediting the customer's account
12. Paying creditors twice and pocketing the second check
13. Appropriating checks made out to cash
14. Raising the amount on checks after voucher approval or raising the amount on vouchers after their approval
15. Pocketing small amounts from incoming payments and applying later payments on other accounts to cover shortages
16. Removal of equipment or merchandise with the trash
17. Invoicing goods below regular price and getting a kickback from the purchaser
18. Manipulating accounting software packages to credit personal accounts with electronic account overages
19. Issuing (and cashing) checks on returned merchandise not actually returned
20. Forging checks, destroying them when they are returned with the statement from the bank, and changing cash account records accordingly
21. Appropriating credit card, electronic bank account, and other electronic data

The Contagion of Theft

Theft of any kind is a contagious disorder. Petty, relatively innocent pilferage by a few employees spreads through a facility. As more people participate, others will follow until even the most rigid break down and join in. Pilferage becomes acceptable—even respectable. It gains general social acceptance that is reinforced by almost total peer participation. Few people make independent ethical judgments under such circumstances. In this microcosm, the act of petty pilferage is no longer viewed as unacceptable conduct. It has become not a permissible sin but instead a right.

The docks of New York City were once an example of this progression. Forgetting for the moment the depredations of organized crime and the climate of dishonesty that characterized that operation for so many years, even longshoremen not involved in organized theft had worked out a system all their own. For every so many cases of whiskey unloaded, for example, one case went to the men. Little or no attempt was made to conceal this pilferage. It was a tradition, a right. When efforts were made to curtail the practice, labor difficulties arose. It soon became evident that certain pilferage would have to be accepted as an unwritten part of the union contract under the existing circumstances.

This is not a unique situation. The progression from limited pilferage through its acceptance as normal conduct to the status of an unwritten right has been repeated time and again. The problem is, it does not stop there. Ultimately pilferage becomes serious theft, and then the real trouble starts. Even before pilferage expands into larger operations, it presents a difficult problem to any business. Even where the amount of goods taken by any one individual is small, the aggregate can represent a significant expense. With the costs of materials, manufacture, administration, and distribution rising as they are, there is simply no room for added, avoidable expenses in today's competitive markets. The business that can operate the most efficiently and offer quality goods at the lowest prices because of the efficiency of its operation will have a huge advantage in the marketplace. When so many companies are fighting for their economic lives, there is simply no room for waste—and pilferage is just that.

Moral Obligation to Control Theft

When we consider that internal theft accounts for at least twice the loss from external theft (that is, from burglars, armed robbers, and shoplifters combined), we must be impressed with the scope of the problem facing today's businesspeople. Businesses have a financial obligation to stockholders to earn a profit on their investments. Fortunately, steps can be taken to control internal theft. Setting up a program of education and control that is vigorously administered and supervised can cut losses to relatively insignificant amounts.

It is also important to observe that management has a moral obligation to its employees to protect their integrity by taking every possible step to avoid presenting open opportunities for pilferage and theft that would tempt even the most honest people to take advantage of the opportunity for gain by theft.

This is not to suggest that each company should assume a paternal role toward its employees and undertake their responsibilities for them. It is to suggest strongly that the company should keep its house sufficiently in order to avoid enticing employees to acts that could result in great personal tragedy as well as in damage to the company.

Employment History and Reference Checking

The key to reducing internal theft is the quality of employees employed by the facility. The problem, however, will not be eliminated during the hiring process, no matter how carefully and expertly selection is made. Systems of theft prevention and programs of employee motivation are ongoing efforts that must recognize that elements of availability, susceptibility, and opportunity are dynamic factors in a constant state of flux. The initial approach to the problem, however, starts at the beginning—in the very process of selecting personnel to work in the facility. During this process, a knowledgeable screener who is aware of what to look for in the employment application or résumé can develop an enormous amount of vital information about the prospective employee. Some answers are not as obvious as they once were, and the ability to perceive and evaluate what appears on the application or résumé is more important than ever as applications become more restrictive in what they can ask.

The increased focus on screening and background checks over the past decade is a direct result of the following:

- A rise in lawsuits from negligent hiring
- An increase in child abuse reporting and abductions, which have resulted in new laws that require criminal background checks for anyone who works with children, including volunteers
- September 11, 2001, resulted in heightened security and required identity verification

- The Enron scandal increased scrutiny of corporate executives, officers, and directors
- Increasing use of inflated and fraudulent résumés and applications
- New federal and state laws requiring background checks for certain jobs, for example, armored car employees
- The Information Age added to the increase in checks because information is now available through many computer databases

Privacy legislation coupled with fair employment laws drastically limit what can be asked on employment application forms. The following federal legislation relates directly to hiring and dealing with employees:

- Title VII of the Civil Rights Act of 1964
- Pregnancy Discrimination Act of 1978
- Executive Order 11246 (Affirmative Action)
- Age Discrimination in Employment Act of 1967
- National Labor Relations Act
- Rehabilitation Act of 1973
- Vietnam Era Veterans' Readjustment Assistance Act of 1974
- Fair Labor Standards Act of 1938 (Wage and Hour Law)
- Federal Wage Garnishment Law
- Occupational Safety and Health Act of 1970
- Immigration Reform and Control Act of 1986
- Employee Polygraph Protection Act of 1988
- Consolidated Omnibus Reconciliation Act of 1985 (COBRA)
- Worker Adjustment and Retraining Notification Act (Plant Closing Law)
- EEOC Sexual Harassment Guidelines
- Americans with Disabilities Act of 1990 (for a more complete list, see Table 12.1)
- Family Educational Rights and Privacy Act (FERPA)
- Bankruptcy Act
- Fair Credit Reporting Act (FCRA)
- Equal Pay Act 1963
- Privacy Act of 1976

In some respects, these regulations had a streamlining effect, eliminating irrelevant questions and confining questions exclusively to those matters relating to the job applied for. The subtler kinds of discrimination on the basis of age, sex, and national origin have been largely eliminated from the employment process. In making these changes to protect the applicant, state and federal laws have created new dilemmas for employers and their security staffs.

Table 12.1 Who is Protected, Who is Affected? Federally Covered Employers and Protected Classes

Legislation	Race/Color	National	Origin/ Ancestry	Sex	Religion	Age	Disabled	Union	Covered Employers	Federal Agency
Title VII Civil Rights Act	X	X	X	X					Employers with 15+ EEs; unions, employment agencies	EEOC
Equal Pay Act (EPA) as amended			X						Minimum wage law coverage ("administrative employees" not exempted)	EEOC
ªAge Discrimination in Employment Act (ADEA)						X	40+		20+ EEs (unions with 25+ members), employment agencies	EEOC
*Age Discrimination Act of 1975 (ADA)						X			Receives federal money	EEOC
*Executive Order 11246.11141	X	X		X	X	X			All federal contractors and subcontractors	OFCCP
*Title VI Civil Rights Act	X	X		X	X				Federally-assisted program or activity—public schools and colleges also covered by Title IX	Funding Agency and EEOC

Law						Covered employers	Enforcement agency
*Rehabilitation Act of 1973				X		Receives federal money: federal contractor, $2,500+	OFCCP
National Labor Relations Act (NLRA)	X	X	X			ER in interstate commerce	NLRB
Civil Rights Act of 1866			X			All employers	Courts
Civil Rights Act of 1871	X				X	Private employers usually not covered	EEOC
Revenue Sharing Act of 1972	X		X	X	X	State and local governments that receive federal revenue sharing funds	OFCCP
Education Amendments of 1972 Title IX					X	Educational institutions receiving federal financial assistance	Dept. of Education
Vietnam Era Vets Readjustment Act—1974			X			Government contractors—$10,000+	OFCCP
Pregnancy Discrimination Act of 1978	X				X	All employers 15+EEs	EEOC–OFCCP

Continued

Table 12.1 Who is Protected, Who is Affected? Federally Covered Employers and Protected Classes—cont'd

Legislation	Race/Color	National Origin/Ancestry	Sex	Religion	Age	Disabled	Union	Covered Employers	Federal Agency
Fair Labor Standards Act	Includes minimum wage law and equal pay act with DOL complex method of coverage								
*Rehabilitation Act of 1973						X		Receives federal money: federal contractor, $2,500+	OFCCP
Americans with Disabilities Act of 1990						X		Covers employers with 15 or more employees	EEOC
Federal Privacy Act of 1976								Federal agencies only	
Freedom of Information Act								Federal agencies only	
Family Educational Rights and Privacy Act								Schools, colleges, and universities, federally assisted	
Immigration Reform Act of 1986								All employers	INS

EE = Employee; ER = Employer; EEOC = Equal Employment Opportunity Commission; OFCCP = Office Federal Contract Compliance Programs; NLRB = National Labor Relations Board; DOL = Department of Labor; INS = Immigration and Naturalization Service.
* Applies to federal agencies, contractors, or assisted programs only.
a Mandatory retirement eliminated except in special circumstances.

Various federal and state laws prohibit criminal justice agencies (police departments, courts, and correctional institutions) from providing information on certain criminal cases to noncriminal justice agencies (for example, private security firms or human resources departments). The Fair Credit Reporting Act requires that a job applicant must give written consent to any credit bureau inquiry.

All states have some type of privacy legislation meeting the guidelines set forth in the Federal Privacy Act of 1976. The most controversial portion of the Act states "that information shall only be used for law enforcement and criminal justice and other lawful purposes." The crux of the issue is the way that "other lawful purposes" is defined. Does this meaning include human resources departments and private security operations? The verdict is mixed. Human resources, security, and loss-prevention operations must be aware of the interpretation of the privacy legislation in each state in which they operate. Recent legislation regarding the Department of Homeland Security has allowed for greater access of government agencies and private security firms to criminal histories, financial records and medical records.

Understandably, there is some confusion regarding the rules governing employment screening. In spite of such confusion, the pre-employment inquiry remains one of the most useful security tools employers can use to shortstop employee dishonesty and profit drains. Security management should consult with legal counsel to determine which laws relate to their locality and establish firm and precise policies regarding employment applications and hiring practices. An employer should be as familiar as possible with the federal Fair Credit Reporting Act (FCRA), which governs what employers must do when contracting record checks with third parties.

Generally speaking, look for and be wary of applicants who:
- Show signs of instability in personal relations
- Lack job stability; a job hopper does not make a good job candidate
- Show a declining salary history or are taking a cut in pay from the previous job
- Show unexplained gaps in employment history
- Are clearly overqualified
- Are unable to recall or are hazy about names of supervisors in the recent past or who forget their address in the recent past

In general, all or some of the following information might be included in a background check:
- Driving records
- Vehicle registration

- Credit reports
- Criminal records
- Social Security number
- Educational records
- Court records
- Workers' compensation
- Bankruptcy
- Character references
- Neighbor interviews
- Medical records
- Property ownership
- Military records
- State licensing
- Drug tests
- Past employment
- Personal references
- Arrest records
- Sex offense lists

If the job applied for is one that involves handling funds, it is advisable to get the applicant's consent to make a financial inquiry through a credit bureau. Be wary if such an inquiry turns up a history of irresponsibility in financial affairs, such as living beyond one's means.

Application forms should ask for a chronological listing of all previous employers in order to provide a list of firms to be contacted for information on the applicant as well as to show continuity of career. Any gaps could indicate a jail term that was "overlooked" in filling out the application. When checking with previous employers, verify dates on which employment started and terminated.

References submitted by the applicant must be contacted, but they are apt to be biased. After all, since the person being investigated submitted these references' names, they are not likely to be negative or hostile. It is important to contact someone—preferably an immediate supervisor—at each previous job. Such contact should be made by phone or in person.

The usual and easiest system of contact is by letter or, in recent years, by email, but this leaves much to be desired. The relative impersonality of these forms of communication, especially one in which a form or evaluation is to be filled out, can lead to generic and essentially uncommunicative answers. Because many companies as a matter of policy, stated or implied, are reluctant to give someone a bad reference except in the most extreme circumstances, a written reply to a letter will sometimes be misleading.

As noted, over the past several years the letter has often been replaced with an email. However, the pitfalls of the letter apply to email as well, yet the ease of use and virtually no cost benefits often put this form of reference check at the top of many budget-conscience managers' preferred means of contact.

On the other hand, phone or personal contacts may become considerably more discursive and provide shadings in the tone of voice that can be important. Even when no further information is forthcoming, this method may indicate when a more exhaustive investigation is required.

REVIEW QUESTIONS

1. Do you need to have videos to support your claim of a criminal act being committed prior to conducting your interview?
2. If the employee is successful at stealing, will they continue to steal?
3. Does the size of the company determine whether they will suffer losses from internal theft?
4. Can anyone fulfill the ideal of total honesty?
5. Can anyone recognize a potentially dishonest employee?
6. By looking at a fraud triangle, what 3 elements are usually present when an employee steals?
7. What do many experts agree is the most important deterrent to internal theft?
8. What percentage of business failure was reported in 2007 as a result of employee dishonesty?
9. Is theft of any kind by employees contagious and how does it affect general employee conduct?
10. How much higher is internal theft compared to external theft?
11. What is the single most key to reducing internal theft?
12. What federal act governs what employers must do when contracting record checks with third parties?

CHAPTER 13

Investigative Interviewing: One Hundred Things You Should Know

1. Be confident.
2. Be positive.
3. Research the background of the interviewee.
4. Do online research of all details.
5. Know your purpose.
6. Control your comfort zone.
7. Tailor your demeanor.
8. Admit to mistakes.
9. Eliminate possible answers.
10. Maintain high professional standards.
11. Use the skills you've developed.
12. Be ready for denial.
13. Have a conversation.
14. Try to develop something in common with the interviewee when necessary.
15. Assess the interviewee.
16. Stay calm.
17. Be adversarial when necessary, perhaps if working with another interviewer.
18. Be adaptable.
19. Know yourself.
20. Know your biases.
21. Expect the unexpected.
22. Control the interview.
23. Properly handle confidential informants.
24. Know the respective laws.
25. Know your company policies.
26. Know the interviewee's rights.
27. Understand your limits.
28. Help subjects recall events.

29. Use props if you have them.
30. Consider the time of day for your interview.
31. Listen and avoid questions that have a yes-or-no reply.
32. Protect any and all evidence.
33. Maintain confidentiality.
34. Be ready for rationalizations.
35. Be empathetic.
36. Observe, attentive, and concentrate.
37. Be alert.
38. Be mentally prepared.
39. Don't have a timeframe to end the interview.
40. Confirm simple details.
41. Have necessary documents.
42. Have questions ready and be ready to take a statement.
43. Be flexible and objective.
44. Always assume there is more information.
45. Observe body language and body posture movements.
46. Set baseline for nervousness by asking innocuous questions.
47. Compare and contrast body language when answering innocuous questions and incriminating ones.
48. Only use Miranda when subject is not free to go.
49. Keep an open mind.
50. Don't keep time.
51. Have a private location.
52. Select the location yourself.
53. Know when to shut up and be silent.
54. Prepare the seating arrangement prior to the interview.
55. Start with small talk.
56. Use deception sparingly.
57. Set the room so your comfortable level.
58. Establish common ground.
59. Know when to stop, pause, be silent, and be direct and indirect.
60. Take notes and bring a notebook.
61. Know when to get help or call an expert.
62. Dare to ask tough questions.
63. Choose questions wisely.
64. Avoid third-degree questioning.
65. Ask closed questions when necessary.
66. Ask open-ended questions when needed.

67. Keep questions simple.
68. Hide your personal values.
69. Maintain a neutral stance.
70. Be patient and break the interviewee's pat story.
71. Control personal anger.
72. Avoid using coercive behaviors.
73. Be nonjudgmental.
74. Use active listening skills.
75. Consider the human needs of the interviewee.
76. Be respectful.
77. Build trust.
78. Be flexible with your methods.
79. Be creative; think outside the box.
80. Let the interviewee talk.
81. Develop a rapport.
82. Watch for behavioral clues such as gestures, facial expressions, and tone of voice.
83. Follow your instincts.
84. Wait till you have enough leverage before you hit that home run.
85. Know when to be aggressive.
86. Practice, practice, and practice.
87. Wear a suit and tie when it might be warranted.
88. Dress casually if it fits the interview setting and style.
89. Control personal anger.
90. Maintain a neutral stance.
91. Apply flexible methods.
92. Cover suspiciousness.
93. Manage your time.
94. Remember the 14th Amendment regarding due process and equal protection.
95. Remember the importance of a well-written report.
96. Use benchmarking.
97. Remember your code of ethics.
98. Use professional conduct.
99. Validate information.
100. Don't get sucked into the trap of familiarity.

CONCLUSION

The investigative interview is an art because each of us makes it such. Each of you will bring your own style, technique, and personality to each of your interviews.

It is my hope that something in this book will help you examine your own values, beliefs, ethics, and behavior and will help you to be a successful interviewer. Remember to treat everyone with respect and work on building relationships that allow for dialogue.

The most powerful advice that I can give to you is to practice, practice, and practice and to embrace your art.

REFERENCES

Anastasi, J., 2003. The New Forensics: Investigating Corporate Fraud and the Theft of Intellectual Property. Wiley, Hoboken, NJ.

Barefoot, J.K., 1990. Employee Theft Investigation, second ed. Butterworth, Boston.

Davia, H.R., 2000. Accountant's Guide to Fraud Detection and Control, second ed. Wiley, New York.

Doig, A., 2012. Fraud: The Counter Fraud practitioner's Handbook. Ashgate Publishing, Farnham.

Felson, M., Clarke, R.V., 1997. Business and Crime Prevention. Criminal Justice Press, Monsey, NY.

Fischer, R., Halibozek, E., 2013. Introduction to Security, nineth ed. Elsevier, Amsterdam.

Fischer, R.J., Green, G., 2004. Introduction to Security, seventh ed. Butterworth-Heinemann, Amsterdam.

Fischer, R.J., Halibozek, E.P., 2013. Introduction to Security, nineth ed. Butterworth-Heinemann, Waltham, Mass.

Friedrichs, D.O., 2010. Trusted Criminals: White Collar Crime in Contemporary Society, fourth ed. Wadsworth Cengage Learning, Belmont.

Gordon, N.J., Fleisher, W.L., 2011. Effective Interviewing and Interrogation Techniques, third ed. Academic Press, Burlington, MA.

Harrendorf, S., Heiskanen, M., Malby, S., 2010. International Statistics on Crime and Justice. European Institute for Crime Prevention and Control, affiliated with the United Nations (HEUNI), Helsinki.

Herlihy, B., Corey, G., 2006. Ethics Surrounding Interviewing, sixth ed. American Counseling Association, Alexandria, VA.

Hewlett-Packard's pretexting scandal: hearing before the Subcommittee on Oversight and Investigations of the Committee on Energy and Commerce, House of Representatives, 109th Congress, second session, September 28, 2006. 2006. US GPO, Washington.

August 1999, The review of metaphysics. J. Philos. 96 (8), (Bibliography), XCIV, 9, September 1, 1997.

Killinger, B., 2007. Integrity: Doing the Right Thing for the Right Reason. McGill-Queen's University Press, Montreal.

Lord, V.B., Cowan, A.D., 2011. Interviewing in Criminal Justice: Victims, Witnesses, Clients, and Suspects. Jones and Bartlett, Sudbury, MA.

Lyman, M.D., 1999. Criminal Investigation: The Art and the Science, second ed. Prentice Hall, Upper Saddle River, NJ.

Luftig, J.T., Ouettette, S., May 3, 2009. The Decline of Ethical Behavior in Business.

Matsumoto, D.H., 2011, June 1. Evaluating truthfulness and detecting deception. The FBI Law Enforcement Bulletin. 1, 1.

Mendell, R.L., 1997. How to Conduct Business Investigations and Competitive Intelligence Gathering. Thomas Investigative Publications, Austin, TX.

Mesis, J., 2005, February. The FTC pretexting. PI Magazine, 43, 0.

Milne, R., 2009. International Developments in Investigative Interviewing. Willan, Cullompton, Devon.

Pretexting: Your personal information revealed, 2006. Federal Trade Commission, Bureau of Consumer Protection, Washington, DC.

Proctor, M., 2003. How to Stop a Stalker. Prometheus Books, Amherst, NY.

Professional and Ethical Conduct, 2001. Introduction to Private Investigation. Reprint. British Columbia: Private Investigators Association of BC, 2005, 10–12. Print.

Royal, R.F., Schutt, S.R., 1976. The Gentle art of Interviewing and Interrogation: A Professional Manual and Guide. Prentice-Hall, Englewood Cliffs, NJ.

Tyska, L.A., Fennelly, L.J., 1999. Investigations: 150 Things you Should Know. Butterworth-Heinemann, Boston.

Williamson, B.M., 2009. International Developments in Investigative Interviewing. Willan, Cullompton Devon.

Yeschke, C.L., 2003. The art of Investigative Interviewing: A Human Approach to Testimonial Evidence, second ed. Butterworth-Heinemann, Amsterdam.

Zaenglein, N., 1998. Disk Detective: Secrets you Must Know to Recover Information from a Computer. Paladin Press, Boulder, CO.

Zulawski, D.E., Wicklander, D.E., 2002. Practical Aspects of Interview and Interrogation, second ed. CRC Press, Boca Raton, FL.

Laws, n.d. Code of Ethics. California Association of Licensed Investigators. Retrieved February 18, 2013, from www.cali-pi.org/?Ethics.

Sebastian, E., Yahoo! March 22, 2011. Retrieved June 23, 2013, from http://yahoo.com.

Jeffery T. Luftig and Steven Ouettette, May 3, 2009, The Decline of Ethical Behavior in Business http://www.qualitydigest.com/magazine/2009/may/article/decline-ethical-behavior-business.html#

INDEX

Note: Page numbers followed by *f* indicate figures.

CPSIA information can be obtained
at www.ICGtesting.com
Printed in the USA
FFHW010044310819
54650641-60340FF